Treasures of Darkness

Finding God
When Hope Is Hidden

Tara Soughers

Nashville
Abingdon Press

TREASURES OF DARKNESS
FINDING GOD WHEN HOPE IS HIDDEN

Copyright © 2009 by Abingdon Press

This book is printed on acid-free paper.

Library of Congress Cataloging-in-Publication Data

Soughers, Tara, 1961-
  Treasures of darkness : finding God when hope is hidden / Tara Soughers.
    p. cm.
  ISBN 978-0-687-65543-4 (pbk. : alk. paper)
  1. Hope—Biblical teaching. 2. Consolation. 3. Spirituality—Biblical teaching.
4. Bible—Criticism, interpretation, etc. I. Title.

  BS680.H7S68 2009
  242'.4—dc22

                                                                      2009005574

09 10 11 12 13 14 15 16 17 18—10 9 8 7 6 5 4 3 2 1
MANUFACTURED IN THE UNITED STATES OF AMERICA

To my family—Mike, Arielle, and Gregory—who have traveled with me through darkness and light

I will give you the treasures of darkness
    and riches hidden in secret places,
so that you may know that it is I, the LORD,
    the God of Israel, who call you by your name.
                                    —*Isaiah 45:3*

Contents

Contents

Discovering Treasures of Darkness

(Isaiah 45:3)

Like most people, I have tried to avoid times of darkness. In the midst of darkness, it can be difficult to see anything worth celebrating. Perhaps it is only by looking back over my times of darkness that I have come to see the promise that God gave first to Cyrus in the book of Isaiah, "I will give you the treasures of darkness, and riches hidden in secret places, so that you may know that it is I, the LORD, the God of Israel, who call you by name" (Isaiah 45:3). Although I might not have recognized them, each of my times of darkness had treasures and riches.

I was in my last semester of seminary. It should have been a time of great excitement and anticipation. Soon I would be finishing three intense years of study. Soon I would be ordained a deacon, and the grueling process toward ordination would end. Soon I would reach the goal that had been my almost single-minded focus for the last six or seven years. It should have been a time of great brightness but instead it was a time of great darkness.

While my classmates began their excited preparations for what would happen to them after seminary, I had no idea what I would be doing. Although by 1990 women in the Episcopal Church had been being ordained for sixteen years, I was sponsored by a diocese that had just begun to consider women for the priesthood. At that point, there was one and only one woman priest in my diocese. There were three other candidates from that diocese who were also graduating at the same time as me, one other woman and two men. Both men were placed in positions in the diocese. Neither the other woman nor I were. In fact, neither the other woman nor I were even allowed to interview for the available positions in our diocese. I didn't find out they existed until after they were filled by the men. We were released to find positions where we could.

But if my diocese was unique in not being able to place more than one woman, it was not unique in having more women than it could place. Searching for a position as a newly ordained woman in 1990 was a nightmare. Over and over again people in other dioceses gave me their regrets, explaining that they were having trouble placing their own women. Or I would hear that if I was really as good as I seemed to be my own diocese would have found a place for me, so there must be something wrong with me.

It was a time of great darkness. At graduation, the names of my classmates were listed along with their new positions, but I was one of the few who had no position next to my name. As my classmates celebrated the end of seminary and the beginning of their ordained ministries, I mourned an end with no beginning in sight.

In those last few weeks of seminary, it was difficult to be around my classmates and to hear of their plans for their futures. I suspect that it was equally hard for them to have me around. Blessedly, some of my classmates were wonderfully pastoral. Even in the midst of their joy, they made space to be with me in my pain. However, others did not.

I vividly remember one encounter with a classmate. He had stopped me to ask how things were going, and I was honest. He listened only a short time before starting to lecture me. He told me that I had no right to feel the way that I was feeling. If I truly had faith, none of these problems should upset me. For him, darkness and faith were incompatible. Darkness was a sign of a lack of faith. After talking with him, I felt worse than ever.

My experience during seminary has not been the only time of darkness that I have encountered. If darkness is a sign of absent or insufficient faith, then I am indeed guilty as charged. I wondered at times if my fellow seminarian was right, if there was something wrong with me. Maybe it was true that I lacked sufficient faith but I think that it is in the darkness that I really learned what it meant to be faithful.

But the strange thing is that these times of darkness, as difficult and painful as they were, have also been times of great growth in my faith. I much prefer the times of great light and great joy that have also been a part of my faith journey, but I think that they have not contributed to my growth nearly as much as the times of darkness. Those times of darkness have been faith-filled.

I don't always recognize my times of darkness as grace-filled as I experience them. I certainly didn't during that last semester in seminary. There are times when God seems absent in the darkness. There are times when I feel lost and even abandoned. But my journeys through the darkness have revealed God to me in ways that I could never have imagined.

And I have found that I am not alone in experiencing God in the darkness. As I thought through the stories of the Bible, I found many in which darkness plays a major role. Although the darkness of these stories can be threatening and frightening, it also holds many hidden treasures. It is reassuring to see such treasures in the Bible stories and to recognize them in my experience as well.

When my seminary colleague took me to task, I did point out that Jesus suffered his own darkness. In the garden of Gethsemane he prayed that the cup should pass him by, and on the cross he cried out that God had forsaken him. If that isn't darkness, I don't know what darkness is. And by all accounts in the Christian tradition, Jesus was considered faithful to the end.

Perhaps it is in those times of darkness that we are given a glimpse of what it means to be really faithful. In the darkness, our faithfulness is not due to the wonderful gifts that God has given us. It is not even due to the hope of what might happen in the future, for we cannot see a future. In the darkness, our faithfulness comes out of a love that expects no reward. Surely, God cannot help but honor such a gift. Great faith does not require that we pretend to be happy in all circumstances but to journey on in easy times and in difficult ones to the One who calls us in light and in darkness.

In the darkness, there are many possibilities and many gifts, but traveling through the darkness is not easy. Few people choose to enter darkness voluntarily. Like most people, I have fought against the darkness, and I have avoided it whenever possible. I have yet, however, to go through a time of darkness without receiving a blessing.

How can we find those treasures of darkness? In the darkness, it is easy to miss them. As you explore the darkness, may you also become aware of the treasures and blessings that surround each of us, even in the darkest times.

CHAPTER ONE
Darkness Is as Light to You

(Psalm 139:7-12)

Even the darkness is not dark to you;
  the night is as bright as the day,
  for darkness is as light to you. —Psalm 139:12

We were deep underground. The cave tour had been interesting, and at times breathtakingly beautiful, but it was soon to become disorienting. We were gathered together in the middle of an incredible open space. The ceiling of the chamber stretched far overhead, and the walls were almost out of sight. It was hard to believe that we were actually underground. That is, until they turned off the lights. The darkness didn't come as a surprise. The guides had warned us in advance what was going to happen. For our safety, they cautioned us not to move about in the dark, and they promised us that they would not leave the lights off for very long.

I don't normally have a great fear of the dark but I had never encountered darkness like this before. Once the lights went off, there was absolutely no light. There were no shadows, no areas of deeper or lighter black. There were no faint outlines, and no matter how much I strained my eyes, I could see absolutely nothing. It was as if I had been swallowed by the darkness. With nothing to touch, nothing to hold onto, I felt as if I were teetering on the edge of a cliff. I could almost imagine that I was in freefall, even though my feet were firmly planted on the rock beneath me. I don't know how long they left us in darkness but I suspect that it wasn't very long. When the lights came back on, the whole group began chattering. The relief at being able to see was intense.

Complete darkness is rare. In these days of security lights, flashlights, streetlights, and car headlights, darkness has almost been banished. Few of us experience the darkness that makes it possible to study the stars or to see the Milky Way on a regular basis. Most of the time, we can ignore the dark, yet many of us have a deep-seated fear of the darkness, a fear that has been mitigated, but not banished, by our ever-present electric lights. True darkness has become unfamiliar to us, and perhaps because of that it is all the more frightening.

Darkness, however, doesn't have to be so terrifying. In fact, darkness often brings great gifts. In our own lives, darkness brings needed rest and relaxation. Intervals of light and darkness are necessary for plants to germinate. In hot, desert areas, darkness brings a welcome and needed break from the heat of the day.

Even if darkness is unfamiliar to us now, it was a common experience to our ancestors in the faith. Before the era of electric lights, they would have known the darkness that we almost never experience. They would have had an intimate knowledge of this strange and intimidating experience.

And that experience with darkness is reflected in the stories that are recorded in the Bible. Darkness is a common theme, and unlike stories now, in which darkness is almost always sinister or even evil, for our ancestors in the faith darkness was many-faceted. Yes, darkness could be associated with death and evil; but darkness was also the place of promise and enlightenment. Out of darkness came creation, and out of darkness we are reborn. Even more astonishing, darkness could be the place of our encounter with God.

But even when darkness does not always bring evil and suffering, it can be profoundly disturbing. In times past, eclipses were often thought to be signs of God's wrath or of the imminent end of the world. Even today, despite our understanding of the way in which an eclipse can occur, such a darkening of the sun can trigger a profound sense of dis-ease. The closest that I have come to experiencing a total eclipse was in 1984 in Houston. It never got completely dark there, but even though I could still easily see, I became profoundly uneasy as the eclipse progressed. The bright blue sky got darker but still remained blue. The sun still shone in the cloudless sky but its intensity diminished. Everything looked odd, and the effect was unsettling. I could understand how ancient people who had no way of understanding what was happening might very well have thought that the world was ending or at least radically changing.

If the stories in the Bible that feature darkness have a common theme, it is that of change and transformation. Darkness is the time to confront those things that we may not wish to confront. The darkness is the time to see what we have been unable to see while blinded by the light. The darkness is the time of endings and beginnings.

So it has been for me. Some of the most important moments of my spiritual life have occurred in times of great darkness. In the darkness, I have been reborn. In darkness, I have struggled. In darkness, I have been enlightened. In darkness, I have encountered God.

Although there is much in me that still tries to avoid times of darkness, I cannot. For if I am journeying toward the One who made both light and darkness, I need to embrace both the light and the dark. As Psalm 139:7-12 affirms, darkness cannot hide me from the One who made it and who made me.

Perhaps the most common feeling in the various experiences that we collectively call "times of darkness" is a sense of the absence of God. In our times of darkness it can be hard to believe that God is really present. Sometimes it is the sense of God's absence that precipitates the darkness, and at other times we only notice God's absence once we are in the darkness.

In darkness, we cannot see. For those of us who have full use of our eyes, not seeing is hardly to be imagined. Even more than our ears, our eyes are the sense that we use most to explore and make sense of our world. It is difficult for most of us to describe things or people without saying what they look like.

In Madeleine L'Engle's novel *A Wrinkle in Time*, the main characters are transported to a planet where the inhabitants have no eyes. The concept of sight is beyond their imagining. Meg, Calvin, and Mr. Murray all do their best to describe sight but it is an impossible task. When they try to describe the three beings who had helped them, they find that they cannot really do so, except by using sight images that meant nothing to the inhabitants of Ixchel. What Meg recalls about Mrs. Who, Mrs. Which, and Mrs. Whatsit is the clothing that they wore, the way that they appeared. She could not separate who they were from how they looked.[1]

And maybe that is one reason that darkness is so frightening to us. We who are so dependent upon seeing are stripped of that sense in the darkness and we have to rely upon other senses for information about the world around us. Unless we can see we don't feel as though we can really understand and describe our world. We are worried about false steps, afraid that we might be stumbling into a pit or at least heading in the wrong direction.

And, if we cannot see anyone or anything else, it is hard to believe that anyone, even God, can see us. "Surely the darkness shall cover me," the psalmist cries out (Psalm 139:11). In the darkness we are hidden, and no one can find us. In the darkness, we are alone. In the darkness, we can expect no help from anyone, for how can they help us if they can't find us?

When I was a child, we played hide-and-seek in our basement. With the lights turned off, it was extremely dark. It was impossible to find anyone by seeing them; you had to touch them. Occasionally, you would hear a noise that gave you a direction, but most of the time, you simply had to grope blindly around in the dark, hoping that your hand would encounter some part of their body. In the darkness, sight was useless.

And perhaps that is why images of darkness are so powerful and prevalent in religious traditions. Often our faith requires us to learn to rely upon other ways of encountering what is around us. Our normal ways of seeing things are no longer sufficient in this new and strange reality. Like the children in Madeleine L'Engle's book, we need to learn to go deeper than simple sight, and to do that, we often have to be deprived of our normal sight.

It can be a scary process, for how can we possibly move forward when we cannot see? But if we do allow ourselves to explore this new place, we find that our other ways of encountering it are sharpened, and we may learn things about it that we would never have learned had we not been deprived of our sight. In this way, darkness can also be a place of new insight, great creativity, and rebirth.

So it is that the images of darkness in the Scriptures contain the promise of darkness as well as its danger. Darkness is the place of death and of birth. Darkness is the place of struggle and of enlightenment. Darkness is the place of blindness and of encountering God. Darkness is the place of loss and of promise.

As the psalmist discovers, however, darkness is not a place of concealment from God. "If I say, 'Surely the darkness will cover me, / and the light around me turn to night,' / Darkness is not dark to you; / the night is as bright as the day; / darkness and light to you are both alike" (Psalm 139:10-11 BCP). God is present as powerfully in the darkness as in the light, and sometimes God is more powerfully present in the darkness: stripped of our sight, we may be more open to the God for whom "darkness and light are both alike."

If God is in the darkness, then it may be that our avoidance of darkness is a way of avoiding God, or at least of avoiding a deepening of our relationship with God. Staying in the light may seem to be safer, but I have never found staying safe to be conducive to growing closer to God. Darkness, on the other hand, requires me to rely not upon my own resources for safety but upon God. More aware of my need of God in times of darkness, I am more open to God's drawing me in.

Darkness may cover us. It may hide us from others and it may even make it difficult to see ourselves but that darkness may also reveal the One to whom darkness and light are both alike.

Questions for Discussion

1. Have you ever been in darkness that was so complete that you couldn't discern any shapes or edges? What was the occasion and how did you feel about that darkness?
2. Were you afraid of the dark when you were a child? What were you afraid the darkness might be hiding? How comfortable are you with darkness now?
3. In Psalm 139, the writer proclaims that wherever we go, God is present, both in light and in darkness. For many people, however, times of great darkness are more characterized by a sense of God's absence. In the times of darkness in your own life, where has God been? Has the

darkness been filled with God's presence or God's absence?

4. When has darkness seemed comforting or helpful?

Note

1. Madeleine L'Engle, *A Wrinkle in Time* (New York: Dell Publishing, 1962), 172.

CHAPTER TWO

Let There Be Light: Creation and Creativity

(Genesis 1:1-5)

In the beginning when God created the heavens and the earth, the earth was a formless void and darkness covered the face of the deep, while a wind from God swept over the face of the waters. —Genesis 1:1-2

"In the beginning"—the beginning of the Bible, the beginning of all time—there was darkness and emptiness and mystery. In our arguments about whether or not this is an accurate scientific description of the first moments of creation, we have lost the sense of the wonder that these words invoke. It has too often come down to a fight about scientific theories and biblical inerrancies, a fight between twenty-first-century AD science and seventh-century BC revelation.

But was God giving a revelation about science in the time of the priestly writers? There is nothing in the Bible that seems to indicate that the purpose of God's revelation is to explain natural phenomena. Perhaps God doesn't think that revelation is needed to teach us what we can discover for ourselves. Instead, it seems to me that God's revelations are focused upon helping us to understand who we are, who God is, and how we are to relate to God and to other people. These are things that are not so easily discerned through reason. Instead, they are part of mystery.

And it was mystery that I believe the writer of this passage was trying to convey. After the shock of exile, the priestly writer was affirming—against all evidence to the contrary—that Yahweh was the God of the whole earth, and that all of creation was a part of God's plan. This passage is written not in the language of a science textbook but in the language of faith and mystery.

How do you proclaim that everything, absolutely everything, came to be from an act of God? You do this by starting with darkness and nothingness. Darkness covered the face of the deep. Nothing was alive, nothing was moving except the wind or Spirit of God, brooding over the face of the waters, bringing forth life out of the darkness. It was out of the darkness that light came. It was out of the darkness that all that we know came. All of it came out of that Spirit-saturated darkness.

In this passage, perhaps more than in any of the other stories of darkness in the Bible, the presence of God is clear and powerful. Before creation, there is nothing in the darkness to obscure God's presence. There is nothing that hides God's presence, for even darkness cannot hide God at the beginning of creation. In the midst of the void, God is.

In *The Magician's Nephew*, C. S. Lewis describes the beginning of the world of Narnia. When Polly and Digory first arrive, there is nothing. They can see nothing and feel nothing. It is complete darkness, for they have arrived just before the creation of this new world. But they don't have long to wait, for Aslan is at work, much as the Spirit was at work as it brooded over the waters.

> In the darkness something was happening at last. A voice had begun to sing. It was very far away and Digory found it hard to decide from which direction it was coming. Sometimes it seemed to come from all directions at once. Sometimes he almost thought it was coming out of the earth beneath them. Its lower notes were deep enough to be the voice of the earth herself. There were no words. There was hardly even a tune. But it was, beyond comparison, the most beautiful noise he had ever heard. It was so beautiful that he could hardly bear it.[1]

In the darkness, the new world of Narnia was sung into existence.

Whether we think of the Spirit moving over the face of the waters as bringing forth life or of God's creating Word thundering from heaven or of a song of incredible beauty singing life into existence, the point of these stories is to glory in the creativity of God, which is reflected in the marvelous creativity that surrounds us. Whether creation happened through the big bang or not is not of primary importance. What is of great importance is that all of creation came to be through the intention and power of God. Creation is God's masterpiece. And just as master artists begin their creations with nothing except their ideas, so God began in the darkness with only an idea, and out of this darkness, God's great creation was born.

Darkness and Creativity

Although we may prefer to spend our time in the light, creativity is a mixture of darkness and light. One of the most famous photographers of all time, Ansel Adams, developed a system by which he could create photographs that showed an incredible contrast range, from the deepest black to dazzling white and all shades in between. Pure black was necessary for his creativity to be released. I know from my own photography efforts that pictures taken at noon, when the sun is directly overhead and shadows are almost nonexistent, tend to be flat and without life and movement. The play of shadow on a person's face brings out their beauty and their personality. We need both light and darkness.

We need both light and darkness in our lives as well. A life that is filled only with light tends to be lived upon the surface. There is no need to delve deeper when all is well and good. Times of great trial, tribulation, and darkness often cause us to grow and develop. In those times, when we are forced to enter our own darkness, we gain access to unexpected depths.

Perhaps it is no accident that Beethoven composed some of his most glorious work after he lost his hearing. The contrast between his outer life of deafness and his inner life of incredible sound was beyond imagining, yet in that time of darkness he wrote works of incredible light.

How often have we gone to bed with a problem weighing upon our mind only to wake up in the middle of the night with a possible solution? In the darkness of night, in the unconsciousness of sleep, our minds become creative. We dream, and as we dream our minds are free to weave together elements of our lives that we might never consider together when we are awake. In our dreaming, possibilities are discovered, and our creativity is enhanced. Of course, sometimes the solutions are bizarre and unworkable, but sorting through the possibilities is the job of the light. Darkness is the place of creation.

Claiming Our Creativity in the Darkness

A friend of mine owns a cottage on one of the Finger Lakes in New York State. It is a place of great beauty and peace. Every year she offers us the use of the cabin for a week. One of my favorite things to do is to sit out on the balcony after everyone else has gone to bed. I watch the stars and listen to the lap of the water on the shore. The stars can be incredible, as there are very few lights around. Many a night I have seen the Milky Way arching across the heavens over my head.

One night as the full moon rose in the sky, something unusual happened. The moonlight made a path across the water. Of course, the moon shining on water often lights up the water between it and the person viewing it, but this one seemed particularly intense. The path of light looked solid enough to walk on. As I gazed upon it I felt a pull toward that shining path stretching into the darkness. Of course, I didn't actually try to walk that path. I was too awake to trust my abilities to walk on either water or light but that image has remained with me. The image was and is an invitation to explore the darkness, a darkness that can have unexpected paths of light.

I have not always found shining paths in the midst of my darkness. Sometimes I see only glimmers of light in the darkness. At other times the darkness has been as deep and impenetrable as the darkness of the cave. When I dare to enter the darkness, however, I have found incredible riches. In my own darkness, I become more aware of the Spirit brooding over the face of the waters. In darkness, my creativity is nurtured.

God and Creativity

As you read further in the creation story in the first chapter of Genesis, you will find that we are made in the image and likeness of God. "Then God said, 'Let us make humankind in our image, according to our likeness'" (Genesis 1:26). What does that mean? It means that we share something of God, something so important that we reflect God's image and likeness.

I suspect that there is more than one thing that we share with God. We certainly are able to love, and in that we reveal something of the God who is love (1 John 4:8). We think and we reason, and in that we share something with God who orders all things. But we also create, a direct connection with God whom we call Creator.

Out of the darkness, God's Word created. Among the things that God created in this burst of creative energy were human beings, who could continue God's creation. We are each called to create. Some of us create by way of art or music or dance but all of us are called to create our lives out of the raw material that God has given us. We are called to create in honor of and as a reflection of our Creator, and perhaps it is in such creation that we most clearly reflect God's image and likeness. We, too, are called to allow our spirit to sweep over the waters of our darkness, so that we, with the Spirit, may cry, "Let there be light."

Questions for Discussion

1. How have you seen the contrast between light and darkness in a novel, story, poem, musical composition, or work of art?
2. Why do you think darkness is emphasized at the beginning of Genesis? What does that reveal about God?
3. When have dreams been an important source of creativity? What did they reveal?
4. In what ways do you think that we are created in the image and likeness of God? How might it change the way that you view yourself if you saw yourself as a creator like the Creator?

Note

1. C. S. Lewis, *The Magician's Nephew* (New York: HarperCollins, 1983), 116.

CHAPTER THREE

Count the Stars:
Hearing God's Promise

(Genesis 15)

"Look toward heaven and count the stars, if you are able to count them." Then he said to him, "So shall your descendants be." And he believed the LORD; and the LORD reckoned it to him as righteousness.
—*Genesis 15:5-6*

Abram had little reason to trust that God would fulfill God's promise. After all, Abram was old and he had yet to have a child. In fact, he had already given up on the prospect of children. No longer expecting the blessing of children, Abram had chosen another heir, his son Ishmael, whose mother was Hagar, slave of his wife, Sarai. Someone would need to take over when he was no longer around. The family could not survive without strong leadership.

But God came to Abram a second time, again stating the promise of children—and not just one child, an unlikely occurrence in itself, but lots of children, as many children as the stars of the night. It was a preposterous promise.

Confronted with the spectacle of the star-studded desert sky, however, Abram allowed himself to believe. He allowed himself to hope that he would indeed have what his heart most desired. He allowed himself to trust in this promise, which seemed so improbable.

In that darkness, the covenant between the Lord and Abram was renewed. "A deep sleep fell upon Abram, and a deep and terrifying darkness descended upon him" (Genesis 15:12). In this deep and frightening darkness, a smoking fire pot and a flaming torch passed between the pieces of the sacrifice, signifying God's commitment to honor the promise. Nothing was required of Abram; the promise and the initiative were God's. All Abram had to do was to accept, something that is not always easy.

In the darkness, Abram was given a promise. By the light of the stars, this promise was given specificity. By the light of the flaming fire pot, the covenant was sealed. In the darkness, Abram came to believe that what had seemed impossible was indeed possible, and not only possible but sure.

Darkness and Promise

I grew up in Indiana. On clear nights when we were out in the country, there were an impressive number of stars. One time when I was a child, I saw the northern lights. I thought that I knew what a starry sky looked like.

Then I moved to New Mexico. In the desert, the number of stars was greatly multiplied. It was as if the sky had exploded with stars. I could no more hope to count them than I could have hoped to count the grains of sand on the beach. It was such a desert sky that symbolized Abram's promise.

Of course, stars are always present in the sky. Even on the brightest day, the sky is full of stars. We cannot see them with the naked eye because the light of our nearest star hides the lesser lights. Only when the sun is shining on the other side of the world do we get a glimpse of the incredible richness of the starry sky. Darkness is necessary to see the promise.

Daylight hides many things. It hides the stars. It hides the Milky Way. It hides the planets that share our solar system, and although it doesn't completely hide the moon, it greatly diminishes it. It is interesting that it is not darkness but light that hides these things. Too much light can blind us to things around us.

In the light, we do not need promises. Everything seems straightforward and obvious. We can see where we are headed and at least see our immediate goal. Our path lies ahead of us. We don't need to worry. All we have to do is to follow the way that has been marked.

In times of darkness, however, our way is no longer sure. If the path is marked, we cannot see it. We are aware that we need to rely on something or someone else. It is then that promises become more important, for we are then aware of how much we actually rely upon them.

Claiming Our Promise in the Darkness

It might be possible to see a promise in the darkness when that darkness is lit by uncounted stars. The very magnificence of the heavens does seem a fitting promise in and of itself. When we look closely and really see the beauty of creation, it is easier to believe in the benevolence of the One who created it. If God could create all that is, then surely

God can fulfill our much smaller promises. Even uncounted offspring from a couple well-advanced in years seems trivial in comparison to the creation of the heavens.

And indeed, awe has often been my response when I have been outside on a clear night in a dark place. The swath of the Milky Way, with its stars too densely clustered to individually distinguish, reminds me of how small I am in comparison with all that is. It is with gratefulness that I accept the promises of the Creator.

But the darkness that we encounter is not always so beautiful or so inspiring. Sometimes it can also be deep and terrifying, as Abram also found it to be. Like Abram, we can descend into a darkness where no stars shine and no sun or moon gives light. Then, all we can do is to wait for the presence of God. And in that situation, we are reminded that the promise doesn't depend upon us. As Abram discovered, it is God who acts and it is God who makes the covenant. All that we are required to do is to accept what we have been offered. Into the darkness something will burst in, a smoking pot or a flaming torch, blinding us and frightening us and bearing a promise for us.

In this deep and terrifying place of darkness, Abram was given the promise. He was promised what his heart most desired. Not only would Abram have many descendants but also his descendants would occupy the land currently held by many other nations and peoples. His people would be greater than any of the others and they would live from the Great River of Egypt to the Euphrates. The dazzling stars were not simply for show: the darkness revealed the details of the promise. It was in the darkness that the promise became real, enfleshed. It is one thing to promise innumerable descendants but God knew that Abram would need something more concrete, something that he could imagine.

In the starry night, we can believe that God is good. We can believe that there is order in our chaos. We can believe that we have a place, even if a small one, in the vast creation. In the starless darkness, however, we may come closer to God. God is as close as that smoking fire pot passing between the pieces of the carcasses. Likewise, the promises become more personal, more real. In the darkness, the benevolence of God is revealed as God's concern for us, personally. The promises that God made to all are revealed in more specific ways to us personally. In the deep darkness, the covenant between God and us is sealed by God's initiative.

God and Promise

Land, descendants, and victory in battle: the Bible is full of promises that God made to God's people. God as provider, protector, and redeemer is a part of the biblical promises as well. God is a God of covenant. Over and over again God binds God's self to the people. A rainbow in the sky was a sign of covenant with Noah (Genesis 9:12-13). An agreement with David and David's descendants was claimed as an everlasting promise (2 Samuel 7:11-17). Over and over again, we hear of God and promises.

But do we really experience God as one who keeps promises? Often we think that God hasn't kept up God's side of the bargain. We try our best to live a good life, yet tragedy strikes. We work hard, yet we lose everything. We pray for healing, yet the one whom we love dies.

But keeping one's promises is not the same as fulfilling every request. We often imagine God as some kind of cosmic Santa Claus who will fulfill every request as long as we have been nice and not naughty. Or perhaps we see our relationship with God as a business relationship. I do certain things and in return the other party is obligated to fulfill their side of the bargain. Covenant becomes contract.

But God is not Santa Claus. Those who do everything right don't always get everything going their way. Just think of Job, who was the most righteous and upright man of his time but lost everything. Just think of Jesus, who was perfect and yet was tortured and died a horrible death. Following God's will doesn't guarantee that everything will always go easily. Even Abram, promised countless descendants, had to wait a very long time for the son promised to him and Sarai. And he almost lost Isaac when God seemed to want Isaac as a human sacrifice (Genesis 22:1-14). At times, it seems as if God is asking us to sacrifice any hope of receiving our promise.

So what does it mean to think about God as a God of promise? What promises have we received? There are some promises that we all share: a promise that God will be with us, that we will not be alone no matter how alone we might feel, that in the end all will work out according to God's plan, that we will be loved no matter how badly we act, and that we are of great value.

Then there are the promises that we receive through the sacraments. In baptism, we will become children of God. In the Eucharist, Christ will be present in the bread and wine. In reconciliation, we will be forgiven our sins. In unction, God's healing power will be present, even if we are not cured. In confirmation, we will be strengthened for our ministry. In marriage, we will be given grace to live together. In ordination, we will be given the gifts that we need to serve God's people.

But there are also promises specific to each person. Each of us lives a different life with different challenges. That means that each of us needs a somewhat different set of promises from God. How do we discover what God has promised each of us?

For me, God's promises have been easier to hear in times of darkness than in times of great light. When all is going well, I am much more likely to assume that I know what is going to happen. The future seems obvious and clear, and I am much more likely to confuse my vision with God's promise. But in times of darkness, I am shaken from my complacency. When it feels as though the promises that I thought God had made to me have vanished, then I am freed to discover what it really is that God is promising me. In such times, my life can turn in a completely new direction.

When God took Abram out to see the stars, his life was changed. Abram had given up hope of a biological child with Sarai and he had already made arrangements for an heir. God, however, had something else in mind, and in that darkness God's promise became much clearer. It wasn't going to work out the way that Abram thought: instead it would be something much better, something that he had never imagined. I am often quite disappointed when God doesn't fulfill what I had in mind, but like Abram, I find that if I let God give me what God wants, it often turns out to be something much more wonderful.

Questions for Discussion

1. Have you ever been disappointed with God for not keeping a promise? Has God ever done something better than you expected?
2. When have you encountered God in the darkness? What promise or promises did you hear?
3. Have you ever had a sense of God offering a covenant to you? What covenant do you think God has made or might make with you?
4. When have you mistaken your own desires for God's promise? How do you think we can tell the difference between our desires and God's promises?

CHAPTER FOUR
Who Are You?
Overcoming Our Blindness

(Acts 9:1-19)

Saul got up from the ground, and though his eyes were
open, he could see nothing; so they led him by the hand
and brought him into Damascus. For three days he was
without sight, and neither ate nor drank. —Acts 9:8-9

Determined and tenacious, focused single-mindedly upon vindicating God against heretics, Saul was unstoppable. Murmuring threats and murder against the disciples of Jesus, he set out for Damascus. He was an avenging angel sent to clear out the vermin who called themselves followers of the Way. With the full authority of the high priest, he began his campaign. It seemed that nothing could stop him. And certainly the small band of Jesus' disciples in Damascus could not have stood against Saul of Tarsus. They would have been destroyed, as Saul had every intention of doing, except for what occurred on the road to Damascus.

As he was traveling to Damascus, something happened to Saul. A light from heaven flashed in front of his eyes, and suddenly Saul was unable to see. He had to be led by the hand to Damascus. Instead of entering the city as a crusading general in the fight to eradicate the heretics, he came as a child, led by the hand. In that flash of light, he became blind.

But perhaps his true blindness began much earlier. He seems to have been blind to a good many things, even before the flash of light from heaven. He was blind to the working of God in the one called Jesus. He was blind to his own guilt in response to this group, particularly his role in the stoning of Stephen (Acts 7:54–8:1). He was blind to the fact that his idea of protecting God's holiness might not be the same as God's idea. He was blind to his own hatred and arrogance. He was blind to the humanity of those whom he persecuted. He was blind to his own blindness.

So what did God do? First, God needed to make Saul aware of his blindness. Before Saul's eyes could be opened, before he could see what God was really doing in and through the followers of the Way, before Saul could see the Lord, he first needed to realize that he was blind and in need of healing. The physical blindness that struck him was a manifestation of the deeper spiritual blindness that had already afflicted him.

As he needed others to take him by the hand to lead him down the road to Damascus, so he would need to find others to help rid him of the spiritual blindness that was the root cause of his physical blindness. Those very people whom he had come to Damascus to murder were to be the source of his healing.

Darkness and Blindness

One of the reasons that darkness is so frightening to us is that it robs us of our sight. We cannot see to walk and we are in danger of tripping or walking into something. We cannot see other dangers that might be around us. How many of us, as children, imagined monsters in the dark when shadowy or half-seen shapes became frightening? When we cannot see, other senses become sharper. We hear noises that we never noticed in the daytime, and we imagine what kind of creature might make such a noise. When we cannot see, we lose confidence in our ability to navigate our world and to meet its challenges. We become dependent upon others, just as Saul was on the road to Damascus. How often we feel that we are moving forward just as blindly in our lives! The way ahead is often in darkness, and we cannot always see where to place our feet for the next step. We cannot see where to go.

So what do we do in those times of blindness? It is tempting to give up. How can we do anything when we cannot see? Danger exists in doing nothing but the danger seems small in comparison to the danger of doing the wrong thing or taking the wrong route. As long as we don't move we have a chance of coming out intact. In our fear, we can be frozen.

How long are we willing to wait in hope that our sight will return on its own? How long are we willing to stay in that darkness without trying to find a way to move through it? How long will we remain frozen? What do we do when our lives turn to ashes around us and darkness descends? Sometimes this darkness is a sign of depression, a disease that needs proper treatment. But there are other times when the darkness is a sign that our lives are no longer heading the way that we had expected. No longer sure which way to go, we are in the dark. We stumble, unable to clearly see the path ahead.

For many years, I had focused upon my goal of being the rector of a small church. Throughout the long process leading to ordination, I was clear about my goal. It was, at times, a hard process. I experienced some temporary detours and some adjustments in my direction, but through all of it, the end was clear.

When at last I achieved that goal, however, I hit a dark time. My goal wasn't all that I had expected, and I had some difficult times. But I don't think that the darkness I experienced was due simply to the difficulties I had encountered. I think that much of it had to do with the fact that I no longer knew where I was headed. I had achieved the goal that I had envisioned for many years and I no longer knew where I was going next. I had been blinded by my focus, and now that that light had been extinguished, I was in darkness. I no longer knew which way to move.

For a long time, I railed against the darkness. I demanded some light before I went any further. I begged for the blindness to be removed. In spite of my entreaties, my pleadings, and my angry tirades, the darkness remained. All this time, I remained frozen in place. Eventually, I came to accept the darkness and my own blindness. I didn't lose my fear of what the darkness held but when I began to accept the reality that I could not see where I was going, I found the strength and the courage to begin to move slowly forward. The first movements were very cautious and tentative. I tested each step carefully before I put my full weight upon it.

It is true that darkness can hide many dangers but darkness also hides many treasures. I have found, in my difficult times, that darkness has often hidden God. Only when I have been willing to enter fully into the darkness have I found God in those times. Only when Saul was blinded, only when the world around him turned dark, did he finally encounter the living Christ.

God and Blindness

Such times of darkness are not uncommon in our life with God. John of the Cross talks about dark nights of the senses and dark nights of the soul. In both cases, a person is plunged into a time of great darkness. The dark night of the senses is a time of purging or cleansing, preparing us for greater closeness to God. Later, the person may experience a dark night of the soul, a time of even greater darkness, to prepare the soul for an even deeper level of intimacy with God.

Why do we have such experiences of darkness? If God is light, why do we experience such incredible darkness as we draw closer to God? Is God playing some kind of perverse game with us? Is it some kind of punishment for our sins that we have to endure before God will reward us? Has God, our light, abandoned us, leaving us in darkness? Why, God?

According to John of the Cross, we are in darkness because we have been blinded by light. John claims that, as we move into closer contact with God, the increased brightness of God's presence blinds our spiritual eyes, much the way that staring at the sun blinds our physical eyes. Having been blinded by the brilliance of God's presence, we experience those times as ones of great darkness. Instead of being abandoned, however, we are already being drawn ever closer to God.

> It remains to be said, then, that even though this happy night darkens the spirit, it does so only to impart light concerning all things. And even though it humbles persons and reveals their miseries, it does so only to exalt them. And even though it impoverishes and empties them of all possessions and natural affection, it does so only that they may reach out divinely to the enjoyment of all earthly and heavenly things, with a general freedom of spirit in them all.[1]

In the darkness, we lose sight of all of the landmarks that have previously guided us on our way. We lose sight of the path that we had been following, for that path no longer leads us in the direction that we need to go. In order to help us see the new thing that God is doing, the new path in our journey closer to the heart of God, God removes the old blazes on the previous trail. For as long as the former trail is well marked, we will have trouble seeing our new path.

Saul, on the way to Damascus, was set in his way. He knew what his goal was: the eradication of a group of people who were perverting the Jewish faith that he loved and honored. Filled with great zeal for God, he pursued this path single-mindedly. As long as he could see the way ahead he continued, unable to see the new thing that God was doing. As long as he was focused upon his goal, he could not see God in the risen Christ. It wasn't until he was physically blinded that at last he began to see once more.

Overcoming Our Blindness

Blinded by the bright light on the road to Damascus, Saul fell to the ground. He heard a voice asking him a question, "Saul, Saul, why do you persecute me?" (Acts 9:4). Although he had been blinded by his confidence in the rightness of his mission, he heard the voice of the Lord— but it was a voice that he didn't recognize. "Who are you, Lord?" he asked, and Jesus answered, "I am Jesus, whom you are persecuting" (Acts 9:5).

What a shock that must have been for the proud and arrogant Saul! He had gotten it all wrong. In trying to serve God, he had actually been opposing God. In trying to protect God from those whom he saw as heretics, he was killing those who were doing God's work. Far from being a righteous avenger of God's honor, he was a destroyer of the new thing that God was doing.

When Saul got up, he could no longer see. Of course, in one sense, he had been spiritually blind for a long time. After the encounter on the road, however, that blindness became more apparent. So it was that Saul, intent on entering Damascus as an avenging angel, arrived stumbling and led by the hand like a young child.

And even when he arrived in Damascus, the blindness did not abate. For three days he stayed blind. During that time he made no contacts. He didn't pursue any business. He didn't even eat. Blinded, in darkness, Saul waited for what would happen next. For once in his life he realized that he was not in control. The next action was not taken by him but by this strange figure who accosted him on the road. Jesus had revealed Saul's blindness, and only Jesus could lift it. There was absolutely nothing that Saul could do but wait.

Waiting is hard to do. We want so much to take charge. We want to fix things, to make them right. We expect that our lives are in our own hands. We believe that we have the power to make decisions about how our lives will go and we do have enough power to make that plausible, at least in the short term. Some periods in our lives everything does go the way that we want and expect. At those times we are on the top of the world, and all that we imagine seems possible.

But life doesn't stay that easy. At some point, we will be brought up short with the realization that there are things beyond our control. Like Saul on the road to Damascus, our blindness will become manifest, and suddenly we do not dare to take a step forward. We become aware that we are lost. Sometimes the best thing to do when we are lost is to stay still and wait to be rescued. I don't know how many times I was told as a child that if I got lost or separated from the group, I was to remain where I was. I needed to let someone else find me. If I was wandering around while they were also looking, we might forever miss each other. I needed to wait, trusting others to find me.

So it was that Saul waited and eventually he was found by a very reluctant follower of Jesus named Ananias. The Lord came to Ananias in a vision and told him to go and lay hands upon Saul to restore his sight. Although Ananias was justifiably afraid to meet the man who had vowed the destruction of all the followers of Jesus, he was obedient. He went to Saul. Through the mediation of the ones he had tried to kill, Saul was healed of his blindness. The one who had tried to kill all followers of Jesus was baptized in Jesus' name.

In times of darkness, we often need others to help us find our way. When we are lost we need others to find us and to set us back on the right path. To regain our sight, we need the support of a community that can see when we cannot see. Like Saul, we may need an Ananias laying hands on our heads so that the scales that have blinded us may fall from our eyes, and we definitely need a community in which we can rejoice in the restoration of our sight.

Questions for Discussion

1. When in your life have you been unable to see the disastrous path that you have been following?
2. What treasures have you found in your times of darkness and blindness?
3. What has been your experience of God in times of blindness? Where have you found God in those times?
4. In your times of darkness or blindness, who has led you by the hand and helped remove the scales from your eyes?

Note

1. John of the Cross, "The Dark Night" in *John of the Cross: Selected Writings*, trans. and ed. Kieran Kavanaugh (Mahwah, N.J.: Paulist Press, 1987), 204.

CHAPTER FIVE

Why Have You Forsaken Me?
Bringing Life out of Death

(Matthew 27:45-56)

From noon on, darkness came over the whole land until
three in the afternoon. And about three o'clock Jesus
cried with a loud voice, "Eli, Eli, lema sabachthani?"
that is, "My God, my God, why have you forsaken
me?" —Matthew 27:45-46

From the accounts in the passion narratives, it was clear
that Jesus had been aware of the gathering darkness during
the last few months of his life. On the way to Jerusalem, a
place that he and his disciples knew to be dangerous, Jesus
had warned them of his coming death. At the last supper,
he indicated his knowledge that one of the disciples would
betray him (Matthew 26:20-25). In the garden he had
prayed that, if possible, he would not have to drink the cup
that had been prepared for him. In the end, darkness
enveloped him.

Although the disciples might have thought that he was
exaggerating things or was simply being morbid, they did
not know the full extent of the darkness that they would
soon encounter. Jesus would be arrested. The disciples
would be scattered. Jesus would be tried and sentenced to
death. Peter would deny him. Jesus would be whipped and
finally crucified, and only a few of the women would be

with him at the end. All of their hopes would be dashed at the foot of the awful cross.

Nailed to the cross, Jesus was stripped of everything: control of his life, his status, his ministry, his friends, and even his clothes. In that awful moment, he realized that he had indeed lost everything, even his sense of God's presence. His cry from the cross was a cry of despair: "My God, my God, why have you forsaken me?" (Matthew 27:46). It was a time of utter darkness.

But this darkness was not simply a time of darkness for Jesus of Nazareth. It was a time of darkness for the whole of creation. The passion story tells us that for three hours, the last three hours of Jesus' life, darkness covered not only him but also the whole land. The world was losing its Savior, and the death of God's Son blanketed the whole land in darkness.

This is the darkness of utter despair. This is the darkness that comes when it seems that evil and hate have prevailed. This is the darkness that is the absence of any light. This is the darkness that swallows up all that is good and hopeful, holy and loving. This is the darkness of annihilation and nothingness. This is the darkness of uncreation.

Jesus died, and the world was turned upside down. The ground shook. The curtain of the temple was torn in two, no longer separating the Holy of Holies from the rest of the temple. The dead walked the earth (Matthew 27:51-53). For a while, nothing made any sense.

The disciples were scattered and the women were left bereft. Jesus, who had been their rock, was taken away, and it was as if they were in free fall. The world was a strange and frightening place. Without his presence, they no longer knew what to do or how to live.

In times such as this, we cling to any sort of stability. Rules become not a burden but a welcome source of stability. Not knowing what to do, we welcome required tasks. Too numb to think or to feel, we simply do what needs to be done. Somehow, even when we have lost everything that has given meaning to our life, we still live. The disciples returned home to wait out the sabbath, so that they could return to care for his body. It was not enough, not nearly enough, but it was something.

Death and Darkness

In the story of the crucifixion, darkness and death are explicitly linked. For three hours there was a complete eclipse of the sun, throwing the land into darkness. Those were the three hours of Jesus' active dying.

A complete eclipse doesn't happen all at once. You don't have complete sunshine followed by complete darkness. Instead, it gets gradually darker. At first, the change isn't noticeable. It is only after a time that the light diminishes enough that it becomes noticeable that something is happening. In cultures that did not yet have an understanding of the astronomical principles, there was often great fear. The sun, the source of all life, was being swallowed up by darkness. Eventually only the corona showed, casting the land into darkness.

As an image of Jesus' death, an eclipse is a powerful one. Nailed to the cross, his life would begin to fade, and that inexorable draining of his life would indeed mirror the draining of light in the eclipse. As he hung on the cross, his life would begin to be extinguished, and death, like the darkness of the eclipse, would triumph over life.

If life and light are so often joined, so are death and darkness. Our ways of talking about death are filled with dark images. We talk about "going to sleep," "closing our eyes in death," and "life being extinguished." It is true that darkness can be scary because we fear the monsters in the dark but perhaps what we fear most in the darkness is death. Horror stories and scary tales rarely take place in full daylight; midnight is a more popular time. And in these tales, although monsters or ghosts are often a part of the narrative, it is death that stalks the protagonists. In the darkness, they are fighting for life.

In the darkness, our hold on life seems more tenuous. Our energy diminishes, and worries that seemed minor in the daylight take on new power. In the darkness, death is waiting. Maybe this will be the night when we succumb at last. So it is that we learned as children to pray, "If I should die before I wake, I pray the Lord my soul to take." Nothing, not even our own continued existence, seems certain in the darkest hours of the night. We long for the morning light to reaffirm once again that we live.

God and Loss

For those who love, the death of someone close can be a time of great darkness. Any major loss casts a shadow upon us. After bereavement, the light around us is diminished. It is as if we are experiencing our own personal eclipse. It may not be a total eclipse but our world is darkened and strange, and we may have trouble seeing our way.

The women waiting at the foot of the cross were also enveloped in the eclipse that surrounded Jesus' death. Where was God as Jesus hung dying on the cross? Where is God in the midst of our personal tragedies? Where is God when it appears that darkness is triumphing over light?

In such darkness, it is often hard to find God. Even Jesus, dying on the cross, felt that abandonment. "My God, my God, why have your forsaken me?" he cried out from the cross. In the midst of our times of grief, we may feel abandoned. In the midst of our times of grief, we may cry out as well. Can we find God in these times of darkness?

Is God present in these times of darkness? In the midst of the darkness, the answer to that question is not at all clear. Wrapped in our grief, we may be unaware of God's presence. Angry, we may reject a God who allows such suffering. Guilty about the ways we may have treated the one who died, we may believe that we are not worthy of God's concern.

Sometimes we feel that God has abandoned us but at other times it is we who distance ourselves from God, trying to reduce the pain and suffering that bereavement causes. Sometimes, the only way that we can survive our loss is to numb ourselves, refusing to allow ourselves to feel anything, choosing to stay in the darkness.

Facing Loss and Death

In the initial stages of grief, we may not feel anything, even God's presence. We may be too distraught to ask about God's presence. But at some point, if we are people of faith, the question of God's presence or absence will arise.

When Lazarus was dying, his sisters sent for Jesus. They believed that Jesus had the power to heal him. They believed that Jesus loved them. They believed that Jesus would be present with them (John 11:3). All that was needed was Jesus' presence to give the story a happy ending.

But for some unaccountable reason, Jesus tarried; all he gave was an engimatic reason. "This illness does not lead to death; rather it is for God's glory, so that the Son of God may be glorified through it" (John 11:4). When he did finally decide to go two days later, the disciples questioned his decision because of danger to his life. "Rabbi, the Jews were just now trying to stone you, and are you going there again?" (John 11:8). Yet when Martha went out to meet him alone, she taxed him with the grief and anger that lay heavily on her heart. "Lord, if you had been here, my brother would not have died" (John 11:21). Later, Mary said the same thing (John 11:32). Where was Jesus as their brother lay dying? Where was God when they needed him?

Where is God when we are confronted with loss? Although there are cases of miraculous healings, each and every one of us has had some experience of death or other loss. If God had been present, surely it would not have happened! The God who is Creator of everything surely has the power to make everything turn out just the way we want it to. But it doesn't work that way. Even Lazarus, raised from the dead, eventually died. There is not one of us who does not encounter the death of loved ones and eventually of ourselves. We cannot avoid the darkness.

Where is God in the darkness? Strangely enough, God seems to be powerfully present in the darkness. In the story of Lazarus, Jesus was with Martha. He was present, assuring her that death was not the end of love. He was present as he cried with Mary over the death of her beloved brother. He was present, bringing life out of death. Jesus was present but not necessarily in the way in which Martha and Mary had wanted him present. He didn't prevent awful things from happening to them but he was with them in their grief.

Where is God in the midst of our bereavement? God is present, assuring us that death is not the end of love. God is present with us as we remember the love that we have shared. God is present, crying along with us, as we express our grief. Where is God in the midst of our bereavement? God is with us, bringing life out of death.

That isn't always the way in which we want God to be present, of course. Finding new life is difficult in the midst of death, but even in our darkest times, God brings us sparks of new life. God is present in the wordless hug that brings us a sense of comfort, connection, and strength. God is present in those who gather with us to grieve, to weep, and to tell stories. God is with us, sowing seeds of new life, but sometimes the only way to that new life is through the darkness.

Questions for Discussion

1. As Jesus hung dying on the cross, he cried out to God, asking why God had forsaken him. When in your life have you felt that kind of despair?
2. When have you been engulfed in the darkness of losses such as death, divorce, or job loss? What other losses have caused darkness in your life?
3. What has been your sense of God in times of death or loss?
4. Who has been the manifestation of God's presence by being with you and comforting you in the darkness of grief?

CHAPTER SIX

Wrestling with God: Transformation

(Genesis 32:22-32)

Jacob was left alone; and a man wrestled with him until daybreak. When the man saw that he did not prevail against Jacob, he struck him on the hip socket; and Jacob's hip was put out of joint as he wrestled with him. Then he said, "Let me go, for the day is breaking." But Jacob said, "I will not let you go, unless you bless me."
—Genesis 32:24-26

The last time that he had been in the land, Jacob had to flee for his life. He had cheated his brother, Esau, out of what should have been Esau's. He had tricked Esau into giving up his birthright by playing on Esau's great hunger (Genesis 25:29-34). He had deceived his father, so that he might receive Esau's blessing as the elder son. Frightened by Esau's righteous wrath, Jacob obeyed Rebekah's instructions that he should flee his home and live with Laban in Haran (Genesis 27:1-43).

Many years passed. Jacob the cheat, Jacob the trickster, Jacob the conniver had come to know what it was like to be cheated, to be tricked, and to be the victim of other people's conniving. He had been cheated by his father-in-law, Laban. He made a deal with Laban to work for seven years to earn his beloved Rachel as a bride, but it really took fourteen

43

years. After seven years Laban threw the promised wedding feast but he tricked Jacob. The bride was not the promised Rachel but his older daughter, Leah, and not until too late did Jacob notice the difference. In the end, through the conniving of his wife Rachel, he was made an accessory to stealing Laban's household gods.

So the brash young man, able with his cunning to win any prize that he coveted, found that others could match his trickery. The young man who was just a little quicker and smarter than others now found a match in his Uncle Laban. The confidence man was taken in by the cunning of others. Oh, he didn't lose his touch completely. He was to learn more subtle and effective means of getting what he considered to be his but he had to grow up just a little. The world would prove a harder place than he had once imagined.

So it was that Jacob decided to return home. It wasn't a sure bet. He could hardly expect to be welcomed by the brother whom he had cheated. He was putting himself and his family in danger. He had no guarantees but perhaps he had learned that life offers no real guarantees. In any event, he journeyed back, still trying to hedge his bets. Having sent his whole party ahead of him, Jacob stayed across the stream from Esau and his approaching force. If anyone was going to survive this ordeal, it would be Jacob. The first danger came not from the expected assault from Esau but from an unexpected source.

Jacob was to learn that there was no safety, even across the Jabbok. Alone the night before his fateful meeting with Esau, Jacob wrestled with a man who appeared. It seemed a fair match: neither could get the upper hand. All through the night, they wrestled, and it wasn't until day was beginning to break that things changed.

Who was this man? We are not told, probably because Jacob didn't know. There are some hints. The man's concern about the coming light might indicate that he was a demon. Demons were known to attack those alone in the desert. Maybe that is who Jacob thought the man was.

In any case, the man was able to wound Jacob. Putting Jacob's hip out of joint should have shifted the battle to the man's advantage. If they had been evenly matched before, they would be so no longer, but Jacob was unwilling to concede the fight. "Let me go, for day is coming," the man demanded of Jacob, but Jacob refused. Even injured, he was determined to wrest something from the man. "I will not let you go, until you bless me" (Genesis 32:26).

So the man blessed Jacob, but not as Jacob would demand. The blessing was on the man's terms. Jacob was left crippled, and more importantly, Jacob's name was changed. No longer would he be "Jacob," the supplanter, but "Israel." In that action, the stranger asserted his power and authority over Jacob. Yes, Jacob wrested a blessing from God, but in so doing, he was forever marked and changed. The healthy Jacob became the limping Israel. Even Jacob came to realize that he, the audacious schemer, had had a close call. "For I have seen God face to face, and yet my life is preserved" (Genesis 32:30). In that encounter, Jacob was transformed.

Transformation and Darkness

Transformation and darkness are inextricably linked, and many impressive examples of transformation in nature happen in darkness. The transformation of a seed into a plant begins in darkness. Hidden deep inside of the earth, the seed begins to grow and to change, revealing the potential hidden deep within it. Inside the darkness of the mother's womb, an ovum and a single sperm combine to form a fertilized egg. That egg will begin to grow and transform itself into a human being. A caterpillar will at some point form a chrysalis to hide itself in darkness. In the darkness, the wormlike body will be transformed into a butterfly. Each of these processes begins in darkness, and darkness is a requirement for transformation.

And so it has often seemed the case in my own life. Times of transition and transformation have been preceded by times of great darkness. To change from a doctoral student in biochemistry to an aspirant in holy orders was such a time of darkness for me. I had felt a call to ordained ministry for some time but I had put it aside. It just wasn't possible then. I was in the middle of a doctoral program. If only I had known earlier, I might have considered it, but now it was too late.

But that decision turned out to be more complicated than I had first believed. The call to transformation wouldn't go away. It turned out that, as inconvenient and difficult as the time was, it was indeed the right time. As I struggled with this call to change, I felt the darkness begin to descend. With the darkness came all of the fears that it brings: fear of losing my way, fear of hidden dangers, fear of death.

Although I was never in any danger of physical death, the death of my old identity as a brilliant student was happening. The first time that I took Physical Biochemistry I flunked it. I, who had never flunked any class, flunked a class in my major. Suddenly, there was the possibility that I would not be able to continue in biochemistry even if I wanted to do so. I had one more chance to retake the course but passing was no sure thing. I had done the best that I could, and the best, for once, was not good enough.

Like the pupa in the chrysalis, I was swathed in darkness for my transformation. In that time, I was not exactly one thing or the other. I was no longer the up-and-coming graduate student that I had been. I had lost that identity but I had not yet found a new one. My old identity was dying, and the new one had yet to be born. In the darkness, I waited and struggled while the work of transformation was occurring.

God and Transformation

Where is God in the midst of such transformations? In the darkness, God may seem absent or distant. Or at times God may seem a threat to our precarious hold on our old identity. In my struggles, God did not seem like a comfort. There is nothing comfortable about transformation. It requires hard work and it is painful and seems dangerous. Only when we have died to our old identity can something new be born, and the process of dying can be excruciating. Faced with death we see no signs of new life. In fear and uncertainty, we try to hold desperately to our previous sources of security only to discover that they no longer offer any security. We find only chaos and darkness. The only certainty is movement.

And maybe movement provides the first glimmer of hope. The darkness is not a static place. We may feel like Alice from *Alice in Wonderland,* falling down an interminable rabbit hole, but we are moving. Something worse may appear when we hit the bottom but with the movement I found at least a promise that this particular state of affairs would not last forever. Where I was moving, I did not know but I was indeed being carried along by a current toward something.

I don't know at what point I began to cooperate with the movement instead of fighting it. I began by trying to hold my ground. I fought long and hard until I had completely exhausted myself, and then I simply quit fighting, finally allowing myself to be carried along. Eventually, however, I began to cooperate with the movement. I still didn't know where I was being carried. I still didn't even know if what lay ahead of me was new life or further death. All I knew was that I was being pulled somewhere, and if that was where I was going, I wanted to get there. I was ready to face anything, even the demise of my old identity. In the movement, I found the hope that something new could emerge, if only I could get through the darkness.

Being Transformed

Seeing a butterfly emerge from the chrysalis is a marvelous and awe-inspiring sight. For those of us who have not been in the chrysalis, the process of transformation is also nothing short of miraculous. I wonder, however, what the caterpillar thinks as it emerges into the new world. I wonder how long before it really learns to be a butterfly. For me, it took time to learn a new way of being. Having lived so long in the darkness, even the light of faith seemed blinding. After a long time as a caterpillar tucked in its dark chrysalis, I had no idea how to be a butterfly.

After the fight with the man in the night, Jacob was changed, but I suspect that he still had not really grasped his new identity. He was still very much Jacob the schemer. Perhaps Jacob learned a little humility in his fight with the strange man in the middle of the night but he was also reminded how precarious life really is. He wasn't quite the same arrogant young man as he journeyed back to his homeland. He was aware of all that he had gained and all that he had to lose.

Only a very frightened man would do what he did. Before the struggle in the darkness, Jacob sent a servant with a very large gift for Esau: "two hundred female goats and twenty male goats, two hundred ewes and twenty rams, thirty milch camels and their colts, forty cows and ten bulls, twenty female donkeys and ten male donkeys" (Genesis 32:14-15). He instructed the servants to send out each group of animals separately, so that it would become a mighty procession. Not content with one major procession, he assembled a second and a third, as big as the first. Maybe, just maybe, these gifts would make up for all that Jacob had stolen from Esau when they were young. If not, at least it would slow down Esau's advance (vv. 16-20).

But all of those precautions did not quiet Jacob's fear: the next day he prepared for the worst. He divided his family into groups. Faced with Esau, who approached with four hundred men, Jacob prepared for hostilities. Perhaps the struggle with the man in the night had heightened Jacob's sense of danger. Maybe his injury made him feel more vulnerable. Whatever the case, he divided the group to try to save at least some and to provide the greatest protection to those family members whom he held most dear.

Jacob put his wives' maids and their children first to bear the brunt of any attack. Next came Leah and her children. Only then did Rachel and Joseph come. After his encounter with the man, however, Jacob was changed. He now stood between his family and Esau (Genesis 33:2).

But Esau had no interest in attacking the column of women and children coming to meet him. His focus was not upon them, but upon his brother. He ran to meet Jacob, and instead of the expected attack, Esau fell on Jacob's neck, kissed him, and wept. Jacob, expecting retribution, received forgiveness instead. The death he had feared occurred, but it was not the death he expected. In that embrace, the schemer Jacob finally died, and Israel was born.

Israel had to learn about grace at the hands of his brother, Esau. He couldn't buy his way back into Esau's good graces. He couldn't manage to trick his way back into the family. All he could do was to accept the forgiveness. Jacob the schemer couldn't accept grace but Israel could.

Questions for Discussion

1. When have you encountered and struggled with God? Were you left with any marks from that encounter?

2. Think of times of transition and transformation in your life. Which of these times contained a time of darkness? What was your sense of God in those times of darkness?
3. How have you either resisted or cooperated with the work of transformation?
4. When have you had a sense of a new identity or transformation? What helped you claim your new identity or transformation? What has made it difficult to do so?

CHAPTER SEVEN

Listen to This Dream: Enlightenment through Dreams

(Genesis 37:1-11; 41:1-36)

Once Joseph had a dream, and when he told it to his brothers, they hated him even more. He said to them, "Listen to this dream that I dreamed. There we were, binding sheaves in the field. Suddenly my sheaf rose and stood upright; then your sheaves gathered around it, and bowed down to my sheaf." —Genesis 37:5-7

Joseph's dreams would be fulfilled. He would live to see his brothers bowing down before him. Many years later, as a governor in Egypt, he would hold their lives in his hand. But the dreams that he dreamed, and the others that he interpreted, would not immediately make all things clear. The dreams were not a clear vision of the future but simply a glimpse of things to come. The way would be shrouded in darkness. There is no way that Joseph could have guessed from those early dreams how it would come to pass that his brothers would bow down before him. I don't think that he would ever have imagined the multiple betrayals, slavery, and unjust imprisonment that would happen to make that vision a reality. His dreams were the beginning of his enlightenment but dreams have a language all their own.

Joseph began life as the favored son. He was indulged and spoiled by his father, Israel. He would end life as a governor of great power and wealth. Joseph could hardly be excused for thinking that there might be a direct line between the two. Maybe it was the memory of those dreams that kept his hope alive in the intervening years.

Often we know truth at a level below that of our conscious mind. In dreaming, this truth can come more closely to the surface but the truth is often hidden or mysterious. Signs and symbols, such as the sheaves of wheat and stars that stood for Joseph's brothers, abound in dreams. It may be some time, however, before we can make sense of such signs and symbols and of what our dream is trying to tell us. The images in dreams can sometimes obscure as much as they reveal. Nonetheless, dreaming is a powerful way of discovering truth. Dreams can help us make sense of what is occurring and what will occur. Perhaps they can even grant us hope in those times when we see little meaning in the images. I suspect that Joseph held on to those visions of a different reality when he encountered his times of darkness, when he was cast into a pit by his brothers and sold into slavery.

Enlightenment and Darkness

Enlightenment is not always welcomed. The future foretold by Joseph's dreams was certainly not welcomed by his brothers. His insistence upon sharing his dreams and their prediction of Joseph's eventual dominance over his brothers was not only distasteful but also threatening. How else can we explain their selling him into slavery? Even his doting father was not pleased by the image of bowing to his own son.

Often we are not prepared for the truth that is trying to come to awareness in our dreams. During the day, when we have more control over our thoughts, we may be able to block unwelcome truths from coming to consciousness. In the dark, however, we have less control, and as we sleep, these truths can surface despite our unwillingness to see them.

Perhaps that is why dreams are so often a conduit of truth in the biblical stories. The cycle of stories about Joseph showcases the power of dreams clearly, and dreams are found in other biblical stories as well. Jacob dreams of the ladder with the angels (Genesis 28:11-16). The angel of the Lord spoke to another Joseph, telling him not to be afraid to take Mary as his wife (Matthew 1:18-24). After the birth of Jesus, Joseph had another dream in which the angel of the Lord told him to take Mary and the infant Jesus to Egypt because Herod planned to kill the child (Matthew 2:13).

I know that we supposedly dream every night. Some people remember their dreams but most of the time I don't remember mine. I do know, however, that in times when I am in transition or when I am in the midst of some kind of major change or transformation I remember more of my dreams.

One time, when I felt as though I were in a time of great darkness, I dreamed that I was on the shore of an ocean. I could feel the sand under my feet and the waves lapping against my toes. The air was soft, and the water was cool but not cold. I felt that I was being drawn into the darkness, but the darkness was no longer scary but inviting. I had the feeling that what I most needed to find was somewhere in that dark water that was stretching before me. As I began to enter the water, I felt no fear or concern. I felt that I was setting out on a new adventure. Even as the water closed over my head, I felt no panic. Instead I had a sense of being pulled forward through the darkness into a new place.

When I woke I was still in a time of darkness but my attitude had changed. I was no longer fighting it. I was looking in the darkness for whatever it had to offer me. The darkness was still difficult but after that dream I could begin to move through the darkness to what lay beyond.

God and Enlightenment

So where is God in our dreams? Some would say that dreams are simply the results of our subconscious at play. Certainly, there are many dreams that seem to be nothing more than bits and pieces of our daytime activities and thoughts combined in new and sometimes bizarre ways. Many a dream can be explained by some type of conscious anxiety or concern playing in our minds even after we have gone to sleep.

Other dreams may be our subconscious minds dealing with problems or issues that have been too complicated for our conscious minds to tackle. Old unresolved issues and disturbing memories often surface in our dreams, especially those that we try to suppress. They are like apples that bob to the surface even as we try to push them to the bottom of the bucket.

So should we dismiss our dreams as sources of our spiritual enlightenment? According to the biblical witness, the answer is a clear "no." God can and does speak through dreams, just as God speaks in visions, in events, and through people. Perhaps in the night as we sleep, our normal daytime defenses are down, and we can hear the softer voice of God so often drowned out by the noises of the day.

According to Joseph, God is the ultimate source of the interpretation of dreams. When Pharaoh had a recurring dream that none of his counselors could explain, it was Joseph who told him what the dream foretold. Seven good years of harvest followed by seven years of famine was the message of the dream. According to Joseph, not only was the dream from God but only with God's help could it be interpreted (Genesis 41:25-36).

Through our dreams, as through the other aspects of our lives, God is reaching out to us, trying to communicate with us. The message may be an unexpected or unsettling one, as in the case of the baker in the Joseph story, whose dream foretold his death (Genesis 40:16-19). Or it may be one of comfort, as with the case of the cupbearer who was restored to his position (Genesis 40:9-15). It may predict a change in status, as with Joseph's dream of the sun and moon and stars bowing to him (Genesis 37:9-11). Or it may help us see what is happening in the world around us, as in the case of the pharaoh's dream. In any case, our dreams, as strange and unsettling as they may be, may also be sources of great enlightenment.

In the darkness, our rational minds are unsettled enough to allow what is not explicable to exist. In the darkness, things that we could never admit to believing take on a life of their own. In the darkness, we are open to a world that we shut off most of the time. In the darkness, even the whispers of God are audible.

Coming to Enlightenment

He needed to capture someone, in order to save his people. I never knew why that was necessary. The why of something often is not obvious in a dream. I only knew that it was important. I was willing, but for it to be effective I could not go to him—he had to capture me. There was a very long chase scene. I ran down halls and up stairs. I ran through rooms in the darkness, and always, he was behind me, pursuing. I could feel myself tiring, and my pursuer getting closer. I ducked into a room, hoping to hide, only to find that it was a dead end. I hid as well as I could in a closet but I was found and captured. I had my hands tied and I was led away. I didn't know where I was going or what was going to happen next because at that point I woke up. I tried to go back to sleep, hoping to resume the dream. Unfortunately, it did not continue, and I was left unsettled.

For quite a while, it was simply a strange but vivid dream. It wasn't until several months later that I realized that the dream was an image of my spiritual life. I had been running from God and had finally been caught. I was now being led to a new place and I did not know what would happen next. That curious mixture of willingness and fear was a reflection of my ambivalence about the way that my life was moving. What did God have in mind for me?

Although Joseph seemed to have little trouble analyzing his own dreams and those of the people around him, the language of dreams is not always straightforward. I certainly can't explain all of my dreams. I suspect that a fair number of them don't mean a whole lot but are simply the loose threads of my life put together in peculiar ways.

But occasionally, if I am listening, I can catch a glimpse of something deeper. Like the dream of the pursuit, I may not understand its message. I may not even immediately recognize its significance. It may take time for us to become enlightened, but dreams have the potential to communicate truths that our conscious minds may overlook or resist.

That dream stayed with me, providing support and guidance in a time of uncertainty and transition. I had been captured by God, and it didn't matter if I didn't know where I was going and what was going to happen to me: God knew. It was a source of enlightenment and hope in a time of darkness.

Questions for Discussion

1. Have you ever had a dream like Joseph had that seemed to predict the future? Did that dream come true? How did it affect those around you?
2. Describe a dream that has had a powerful impact on you. Why was that dream important?
3. How do we know when it is God who is speaking in our dreams?
4. What has God revealed to you through your dreams? How have you been enlightened through dreams?

CHAPTER EIGHT

Out of the Whirlwind: God as Mystery

(Job 3:1-10; 38:4-21)

"Where were you when I laid the foundation of the earth?
  Tell me, if you have understanding." —Job 38:4

Job had suffered a great deal. His oxen and donkeys were carried off by the Sabeans, and his servants were killed. A fire from heaven consumed his sheep and some more servants. The Chaldeans raided the camels and killed even more servants. A great wind collapsed the tent containing all of his sons and daughters, killing them. Finally he was afflicted with loathsome sores from his head to his feet (Job 1:13–2:8). If anyone had reason to question God, Job did.

His so-called friends visited, supposedly to comfort him, but they were small comfort. With friends like these, who needs enemies? Rather than comfort Job, they added to his misery. They pointed to Job's condition as proof that Job was not nearly so good as everyone had thought. Only a guilty person could have been so cursed by God. Job, however, stubbornly maintained his innocence in the face of their insistence.

And he was indeed innocent, according to the beginning fable. God asked Satan, "Have you considered my servant

Job? There is no one like him on the earth, a blameless and upright man who fears God and turns away from evil" (Job 1:8). Satan, the original skeptic, claims that Job is good because it pays to be good. He has been blessed many times over for following the rules. Satan says that if Job were really tested he would be shown to be flawed like all the rest. So it is that God allows Job to be tested, to lose everything in order to see if Job will remain faithful.

And Job does remain faithful. He never curses God, although he does curse the day that he was born. Even when his wife urges him to curse God so that he might be put out of his misery, Job refuses. "Shall we receive the good at the hand of God, and not receive the bad?" (Job 2:10).

But just because Job refused to curse God does not mean that he was passive in the face of his suffering. Job was not patient. He demanded an answer from God, an explanation for his suffering. If he had done something that merited such punishment, then God needed to prove it. Job wanted a world that made sense but he did not get an answer; he was confronted with a mystery that was beyond his comprehension. The One who made all things is always beyond our comprehension. The world will not always make sense.

Mystery and Darkness

It was a small room set apart for meditation and prayer. A great deal of effort had been made to make it an inviting space. There were chairs and pillows, soft colors and icons. Swathing the room was a long piece of material into which prayer requests could be tucked. Candles were available as well. The window to the outside looked out on a garden. I found myself drawn to this room repeatedly during the week I was at the retreat center. It was a warm, welcoming, and comforting space.

About half-way through that week, though, my sense of God's presence altered dramatically. What had seemed like a joyful, light relationship suddenly became much, much more intense and strange. I was being pulled from what I knew to something else, something beyond what I had experienced before. It was thrilling and exciting, and when I think about it, it was a little scary too. I was being pulled out of the light of what I had known into the darkness of a deeper mystery.

I found that the room where I had been praying no longer seemed to hold the same attraction in the daytime. Its presence at night drew me in. After dark, when the windows were covered and I could no longer see the icons and the cloth around the walls, I could feel something that I had missed in the brightness of the day. I could sense the mystery that now so vividly surrounded me. Sitting in that room, either in complete darkness or with only one small candle, I felt myself enveloped by the mystery of God and of what God was now doing in my life. The darkness put me in touch with that which was beyond what I could describe and grasp. In the darkness, I was aware that I was part of something much larger and more magnificent than what I could see.

That has not been the only time when I have felt a sense of awe at night in the face of mystery. Some of my favorite times and places have been encountered in darkness. For the last several summers, my family has spent a week on one of the Finger Lakes in New York, at the cottage of a friend. While we are there, my favorite part is the nighttime. After everyone else is in bed, I sit on the porch in the darkness, listening to the lap of the water, being enveloped by the mystery. In previous years, the night sky had been full of stars. The full moon cast its glow on the lake, bathing all in beauty. This past year, however, it rained almost all of the time. I never saw the moon over the lake and rarely did I see any stars.

At first I was disappointed because I was surrounded by an inky, impenetrable darkness. But I found as I sat there that I still had the sense of being surrounded by the mystery of God. The mystery wasn't in the beauty of the moonshine. It wasn't in the glory of the stars. The mystery was in the darkness, which enveloped and surrounded me like a blanket. I could not define how I perceived God at that moment, but I was aware that I was indeed in God's presence.

God and Mystery

God is mystery. That is a theme repeated over and over throughout the Bible. Don't make any graven images, the Israelites are told in the Ten Commandments (Exodus 20: 4-6). It is impossible to capture God that way. Don't put your trust in images of wood, silver, or gold. They aren't God, as the prophets reminded the Israelites (Isaiah 2:18). When Moses asked God for a name, God answered, "I AM

WHO I AM" (Exodus 3:14). A name may define us, but we cannot define God. If you think you can understand God, if you think that you can control God, then you haven't really encountered God. God cannot be fully comprehended by us.

That does not mean that we do not try to understand God or that we do not try to define God. Humans have a great need to understand. We want our world to make sense. We want to know. But the way to knowing God is not through defining God or through understanding all that happens to the world. The way to knowing God, as Job discovered, is to enter into the mystery, for only in the mystery will we really be able to encounter God.

Job was demanding to understand. He wanted his world to make sense. He knew of no transgressions that he had committed. Either he was being punished fairly or else God was unfair. In the world of daylight, in the world of reason, those were the only two options that he could see. He challenged God to determine which of those two things was true.

> "If I have walked with falsehood,
>   and my foot has hurried to deceit—
> let me be weighed in a just balance,
>   and let God know my integrity!—
> if my step has turned aside from the way,
>   and my heart has followed my eyes,
>   and if any spot has clung to my hands;
> then let me sow, and another eat;
>   and let what grows for me be rooted out." (Job 31:5-8)

Although God did respond to Job's remarks, God did not choose to respond to Job's either/or choice. Instead, God vividly demonstrated Job's limited understanding of the world, an understanding that cannot really comprehend and define the activity of God. "Who is this that darkens counsel by words without knowledge? / Gird up your loins like a man, / I will question you, and you shall declare to me" (Job 38:2-3). God challenged out of the whirlwind. Instead of entering Job's worldview, God invited Job into the whirlwind with God.

In the whirlwind, Job encountered the mystery of God, a mystery that was far greater than anything that he could have imagined. Images of God's ways swirled around him in the whirlwind. In the story of creation, Job caught a glimpse of God the Artist. In the care in which all things were made and have their place, Job caught a glimpse of God the All-knowing. In the awe-inspiring visions of rain and lightning, Job caught a glimpse of God the All-powerful. In the intricate concern that God has for all living creatures, Job saw God the Lover. In the whirlwind, Job came to know God more fully, yet at the same time, he came to know how little he could comprehend.

Did Job get his questions answered in the whirlwind? No, he didn't. God never explained Job's suffering. God never declared whether Job was righteous as Job claimed or a secret sinner as his friends believed. Job did not get what he asked for; instead Job got something much more important. In the whirlwind, Job encountered the mystery of God, and that mystery satisfied and filled him in a way that no answer would have. Having encountered God, Job was at peace. "I had heard of you by the hearing of the ear, / but now my eye sees you" (Job 42:5). For Job, that was more than enough.

Living Into the Mystery

"Why?" we demand when we, like Job, are confronted with tragedy. "Why?" we cry out in the face of massive human suffering. "Why, God?" we demand when our world seems to make no sense, when it seems that evil is rewarded and goodness is punished. "Why, why, why?" We seek to make this world comprehensible, rational, and just, and if we cannot make it come out just, we would at least settle for comprehensible. If we can understand, even if we don't agree, the world seems a safer place. In the end, however, there is much that we cannot understand, and what little we understand does not fill our souls. Although what we demand is knowledge, what we need is different; we need an encounter with God. We may not get the answers that we believe will set us free. Our whys may never go away. But we will come face-to-face with God.

When we step into the whirlwind, we are given no promises, save one: we will encounter our God. It won't be a God whom we can fully name. It won't be a God whom we can depict through images. It won't be a God whom we can fully understand. It will be a God full of mystery, who is much greater than we could ever imagine. It will be a God whose nature is revealed in the intricacy and mystery of nature. It will be a God who cares enough to come into relationship with us. Like Job, we can then affirm, "Therefore I have uttered what I did not understand, / things too wonderful for me, which I did not know" (Job 42:3).

In the darkness, we become acquainted with the One who makes both the light and the darkness. In the darkness, we find the One who knows the way to the "dwelling of light" and "the place of darkness" (Job 38:19). In the darkness, we will not find answers. We will find mystery. When we do, it will be more than enough.

Questions for Discussion

1. When have you felt a sense of mystery in the darkness? Was it scary or comforting?
2. How have you responded to great and unexplained losses in your own life? What questions emerged for you during these times?
3. If you have not received answers from God during difficult times, what gifts did you receive from God? Did they satisfy you?
4. When have you felt as though you were in a whirlwind? How was God present for you in that whirlwind?

CHAPTER NINE

How Can These Things Be?
Being Born Again

(John 3:1-21)

*Now there was a Pharisee named Nicodemus, a leader of
the Jews. He came to Jesus by night and said to him,
"Rabbi, we know that you are a teacher who has come
from God; for no one can do these signs that you do
apart from the presence of God." —John 3:1-2*

It would have been easier to approach Jesus during the day
but Nicodemus chose to come to him at night. It wasn't that
he didn't believe in Jesus or that he thought that Jesus was
wrong or evil. His first words attest to his belief that Jesus
had come from God. Why did Nicodemus come at night?
Presumably, it was because he did not want to be seen.

Nicodemus was a Jewish leader, a man of position and
importance. He would have had to be careful about being
seen listening to and talking with this itinerant preacher
and miracle worker who wasn't quite respectable. In fact,
Jesus was downright dangerous. According to the Gospel
of John, just before this encounter, Jesus had attacked the
sellers in the temple, driving out the sheep and cattle and
overturning the tables of the moneychangers (John 2:13-22).
In that act, Jesus set himself against the economic base of
the Jewish authorities. He was attacking the system of
which Nicodemus was a part. It isn't surprising that

Nicodemus came to see Jesus at night, when others would be unlikely to see him. It was actually more surprising that Nicodemus came to see Jesus at all.

But something drew this cautious Jewish leader to Jesus; something caused Nicodemus to risk his status and position so that he could talk with the teacher. In Jesus' teachings or perhaps in his actions, Nicodemus saw a glimpse of God. In Jesus, Nicodemus encountered the presence of God. He came, I suspect, not knowing what it was that he wanted from Jesus but feeling drawn to this man who was manifesting such signs of God's presence.

But whatever it was that Nicodemus expected from this encounter, he didn't expect Jesus' next words to him. Jesus started talking about the need to be born from above. A grown man, Nicodemus could not comprehend how he could possibly be born again. The whole idea seemed ludicrous. "How can anyone be born after having grown old? Can one enter a second time into the mother's womb and be born?" (John 3:4). Although entering our mother's womb again is not possible, rebirth is not only possible, but necessary.

Birth and Darkness

Childbirth, of course, can happen at any time of day. I suspect that there are a fair number of people who were born at noon, but it seems, at least from my limited experience, that births are more likely to occur at night. When we are relaxed, when we let go of our consciousness in sleep, then our bodies may be better prepared for the hard work of birth.

And almost the whole of the process takes place in darkness for the baby. In the wet, warm darkness of the womb, the baby is nurtured and grows. Then suddenly, the child is pushed and squeezed. The idyll is broken by the force of the contractions. Unable to see anything, the sense of touch becomes much more acute. The baby is forced through the narrow, dark passage, a tunnel. After a while, there are glimpses of light, the first light the child has ever seen. Finally, the baby is pushed free of the mother's body, where all of her needs have been provided—food, water, oxygen, removal of wastes, protection from disease—into a place of light and of cold, where she will suddenly have to eat, drink, and breathe for herself. It is no wonder that babies scream at birth, for it is a traumatic moment. The dark, which has been a place of nurturing, is shattered. Who knows what this place of light will be?

Perhaps this is one time in our lives when we would prefer to stay in the darkness, for in our early life, darkness is indeed good. Like the butterfly in the chrysalis, babies are first nurtured in darkness. It is not darkness that is scary, but the sudden erruption of light, revealing a world much larger, stranger, and colder than we could ever have imagined. It is out of darkness that we are born.

But we soon accustom ourselves to this new world of light. We become used to evaluating our surroundings by sight, not by touch or taste. We become so dependent upon sight that darkness becomes not comforting but problematic. We lose the memory of darkness as the place we were first nurtured.

God and Birth

"No one can see the kingdom of God without being born from above," Jesus tells the astonished Nicodemus (John 3:3). What could he possibly mean? Nicodemus was a grown man. It had been a very long time since his birth. He was too large to retreat into his mother's womb, and so Jesus' words sounded like nonsense to him. How could one be born after having grown old?

For Nicodemus, birth was a once-in-a-lifetime event. When he first left the womb, he was born, and it was something that could never happen again. Jesus, obviously, had a much different understanding of birth. For him, that first physical birth was but one example of the many ways in which we are born. Something other than a physical birth was needed in order to see the kingdom of God. To see the new thing that was happening, Nicodemus would need to be born from above.

Having birthed two children, I am convinced that God is involved in our first birth. It is indeed a miracle. But God's birth-giving, life-giving, transforming love doesn't stop with that first birth. Over and over throughout our lives, we die to an old way of life, so that we can be reborn into the people that God is calling us to be. Like our first birth, these subsequent births are often painful and messy. Like the first birth, they can be dangerous and scary, but they are also moments of possibility, mystery, and grace. In birth all becomes new, our world expands, and we see things that we never could have imagined.

It may take time to make sense of this new world that we have entered. Newborn babies do not immediately understand the world into which they are born. We spend the rest of our lives making sense of the physical world. As children, we intensely explore and delight in all of its parts, even those parts of the world that grown-ups no longer notice.

So, too, when we are born from above, we are brought into a new world, the kingdom of God. It may seem strange. We may not understand this new world, but we have the chance, like infants and toddlers, to explore and delight in this new world that we can now see for the first time. It is to such a birth that Jesus was inviting Nicodemus, and it is to such a world that Jesus invites us.

Being Born Again

My transformation from a scientist studying *Yersinia pestis* (the bacterium that causes bubonic plague or Black Death) into a parish priest was not accomplished quickly, easily, or without pain. It was a time of great darkness. Even though my previous existence was no longer comfortable, I was in no hurry to leave it. It was familiar and safe, and I didn't really know what lay ahead if I chose to follow the call to a new existence as a parish priest. But like the pangs of birth, the push to leave that womb was strong and inexorable. I was forced out of my previous existence into a whole new way of being and living. I was reborn, and like most newborns, I wasn't well equipped for this new life that was thrust upon me. I was confused and helpless. Even the basics of everyday living in this new world had to be learned. Like a newborn, I complained loudly about the change, registering my shock and disapproval at my birth.

That isn't the only rebirth that I have experienced in my life. Although Nicodemus seems to think that two births is one too many, I have found that God has had to push me, kicking and screaming, into new worlds periodically. Each and every one of these new births has been preceded by darkness, and the coming into the new world is an experience of almost blinding light. Only with that push from God would I ever allow myself to leave the comfort and security of what I have known for the unknown life that was in front of me.

No one can predict exactly when a baby will be born. There are signs that labor will begin shortly but the exact moment is a mystery. There are many home remedies that seek to hurry up this process for those mothers who are tired of waiting. Raspberry tea was one of the recommended possibilities when I was pregnant. It may be helpful for some women but it didn't work when I tried it!

I think that the same is true of our rebirths. There may be signs that something is beginning to happen in our lives. We may feel a pull in a new direction. We may sense the end of our time in a particular situation. But the actual beginning is not completely under our control. We can fight it, trying to delay our birthing, or we can try to cooperate with it, allowing it to come sooner. In the end, though, it is God who finally decides when it is time for us to be reborn. It is God who provides the irresistible force moving us along the birth canal to new life, and it is God who catches us as we are born, even if we do not recognize God's hands.

Questions for Discussion

1. Jesus' call challenges Nicodemus's religious beliefs and understandings. When have your beliefs been challenged, and how did you respond?
2. When have you been reluctant to leave the darkness for something new?
3. When have you felt that your horizons were dramatically expanded? What was your first reaction to this new place?
4. When in your life have you felt reborn? Did those births come after times of darkness? What were the signs that this birth was imminent?

CHAPTER TEN

Gate of Heaven: Encountering God Where Least Expected

(Genesis 28:10-22)

"Surely the LORD *is in this place—and I did not know it!" And he was afraid, and said, "How awesome is this place! This is none other than the house of God, and this is the gate of heaven." —Genesis 28:16-17*

Jacob may have felt that he had also left God behind when he fled his brother Esau's justified wrath. He had left behind all the places where he had previously encountered God and he did not know that God was present in this place.

There was so much that Jacob did not know! Jacob was a manipulative man, intent on furthering his own interests. Finally, his machinations caught up with him, and he was forced to flee for his life from his brother's justifiable anger. Esau had been robbed of his inheritance and blessing by Jacob's deceptions, and Jacob could hardly expect to receive mercy at the hands of the one whom he had been systematically defrauding. So Jacob fled for safer territory.

Away from home, on his way to join his mother's people, he camped out for the night, and while he slept, he encountered God. Jacob, who had always relied upon his own wits, was confronted with One whom he could not con. He was confronted with something much bigger than he had ever encountered. He saw a ladder stretching above his head, rising up to heaven. Angels of God were climbing up and down the ladder, going about their business. For a night at least, Jacob was able to see something of the workings and majesty of God, and perhaps, for a little while, he was reminded that he had only a small role to play in creation. Jacob encountered One who made him look small.

So it was that Jacob the trickster became Jacob the worshipper of God. In the morning he took the stone that had served as his pillow and anointed it with oil. He named the place *House of God* for the vision that he had seen. I think that this is the beginning of Jacob's transformation in this totally unexpected place.

Not that he was completely transformed in this one encounter with God, but at least he was finally moving in the right direction. Even if he was not quite willing to give up control of his life to this God whose messengers lit up the night sky, he was willing to deal with God directly. He offered God a deal: if you keep me safe and bring me back to my father's house, then you can be my God and I will tithe. It was on Jacob's part a straightforward business deal, but it was also his first acknowledgment that there just might be someone greater than him.

Darkness and Encounter

We don't normally expect to encounter God in the dark. Instead we expect frightening creatures, a belief that we enact every Halloween. On that night, we confront the dangerous night creatures: vampires, witches, ghosts, skeletons, mass murderers, monsters, and other horrible and scary beings. Although there will also be a variety of pretty costumes or favorite characters on Halloween, many of those who dress up will go for the traditional horrors of the night. Fake blood and fangs, weapons of all sorts, and grotesque features are prominent, reinforcing the idea that whatever you encounter in the night is likely to be scary and dangerous. "From ghoulies and ghosties and long-leggedy beasties and things that go bump in the night, good Lord deliver us," an old prayer petitions God. In the dark, we imagine all kinds of things but none of them good and none of them God.

So, too, in our times of inner darkness it is hard to believe that we will encounter God. Having encountered so many difficult or horrible things, it is hard to believe that in the darkness we might also find something positive and life-giving, let alone God. Can anything good come out of our darkness?

I suspect that there is a time for most of us when we realize that we have accomplished the goals that we have set out for ourselves, and the result is not what we had expected or hoped for. That was certainly true for me. I really believed that my call to ordained ministry was a call to serving small congregations, and when I had at last reached that point, everything should have been wonderful. But it wasn't how I imagined it. Due to previous events in the congregations, my first two years were hard, very hard. I wondered why God had called me into this ministry and I wondered why I had ever agreed. The darkness descended upon me, and I lost any sense of God's presence.

It had been a long and dark time for me. Even as I slid into the darkness, I had fought it. Nothing in my life seemed to be going well, but I was determined not to give up, not to succumb. I yelled at God. I fought. I demanded answers. I tried through force to hold the darkness at bay, but finally I couldn't manage any longer. The darkness closed in around me. No longer able to pray, no longer able to resist, I waited in the darkness for whatever would come. I didn't expect anything. All expectations had been drained from me. I suppose if I had thought ahead I would have expected more of the same. I certainly didn't expect to encounter anything good in the darkness. But it was in the darkness that I found God.

Perhaps it is more accurate to say that God found me, for I had no sense of movement. In any event, like Jacob, I encountered God in the darkness in a more profound way than I had ever done before.

God's Presence in Darkness

It was a long time before I understood why the mystics seem to write about preferring the dark times to the times of great light. How could anyone prefer the painful and difficult parts of our spiritual journeys to those moments of light and happiness? What twisted logic makes the times of darkness seem to be more important and powerful experiences? I have had moments of great darkness and I have had moments of great light in my spiritual journey.

Although I experience great joy in the times of light, I must admit that some of the most powerful encounters that I have had with God have been in the times of great darkness.

I had been in darkness for a long time, maybe a year and a half. I gave up trying to find my way through it. I was no longer able to pray. All I could do was sit in the darkness. It was a time when I found the story of Jesus in the garden of Gethsemane to be the most meaningful passage of the Bible. I could understand the darkness that Jesus felt, the sense of abandonment and betrayal, and the sense of events being out of his control. I knew about despair, and Jesus' cry, "If it is possible, let this cup pass from me" (Matthew 26:39), resonated deep within me. Unlike Jesus, I didn't know what lay ahead, but like him, I suspected that it was going to be difficult and incredibly painful. How could he accept what lay ahead? That was the one thing that really didn't make sense to me. How could he say, "Not my will but yours be done," (Matthew 26:39, paraphrased) knowing that what lay ahead was the cross? How could he accept his coming suffering?

It was Henri Nouwen's book, *Can You Drink the Cup?*, that finally gave me insight into this mystery. Nouwen says, "The cup of sorrow, as inconceivable as it seems, is also the cup of joy. Only when we discover this in our own life can we consider drinking it."[1] I had never considered that the joy and the suffering were so intertwined that in order to drink the joy, we also have to drink the suffering, that they are part of the same cup given us to drink.

Suddenly, I knew how Jesus could have accepted that cup, and from somewhere deep inside of me, a yes burst forth. It wasn't a yes to a particular fate or a particular request, for I did not know what it was that I was being called to do. Instead, it was a profound yes to God, a yes to life. It was an acceptance of the cup that I was being offered, a cup that contained suffering as well as joy. In that blazing moment of acceptance, I encountered God, who had been present in the darkness all along. My attitude toward darkness changed. After that point, darkness would never be as fearful and negative as it had been before, for in the darkness I had come face-to-face with God.

Finding God

So much of our faith equates God with light, and certainly, there are many passages in the Bible that talk about God as light. That is where we are told to expect to find God. But if God is the God of both darkness and light, then God is just as strongly present in the darkness. The problem with finding God in the darkness is not God's absence but our inability to see God where we do not expect to find God.

Certainly, I did not expect to see God in the darkness and suffering. I did not expect to see God in the cup of sorrow that was before me. I did not expect to see God but God was present, and when I was willing to drink the cup before me, when I was willing to drink the cup of sorrow, I encountered God.

Since then, there have been other dark times, and as painful as they have been, they too have been times of great growth when I have learned to encounter God in new ways, when I have learned to follow and to love God, even when it was not easy. In learning how to love just a little better, I have learned to perceive God's love for me, even in darkness.

As Jacob learned, one cannot encounter God and remain unchanged. In these unexpected encounters something dies, and something new is reborn. For Jacob, some of the old manipulator and trickster, the one who made sure that all would go his way, died and he was brought into a new relationship with the One he encountered.

In the darkness when I encountered God, something in me died as well. No longer would I demand that God come to me in light. No longer would I expect my cup of joy to be unmixed with sorrow. No longer would I fear the darkness in the same way, for in the darkness, I had encountered God.

Questions for Discussion

1. Where do you most expect to find God? Where do you least expect to find God?
2. Jacob encountered God in an unexpected place. Where are the unexpected places where you have encountered God?
3. How has the darkness been a "House of God" for you? What blessings have you experienced during dark times?
4. Have you ever, like Jacob, attempted to make a deal with God? What prompted the deal, and what was the outcome?
5. Have you ever had a sense that you were being asked to drink the cup of sorrow? In doing so, have you found joy mixed in with the sorrow?

Note

1. Henri J. M. Nouwen, *Can You Drink the Cup?* (Notre Dame, Ind.: Ave Maria Press, 1996), 38.

CHAPTER ELEVEN

The Light Shines in the Darkness: God's Self-Revelation

(John 1:1-5)

What has come into being in him was life, and the life
was the light of all people. The light shines in the dark-
ness, and the darkness did not overcome it. —John 1:3-5

In times of darkness, we can despair of ever seeing light again, but according to the writer of the Gospel of John, it was in such a time of darkness that God's light was revealed most clearly. By the time that John's Gospel was written, the early church was experiencing a time of darkness. The final split between the Jews and Christians was occurring. Within the Jewish community, those who followed Jesus were no longer welcome in the synagogues: in fact, there were anathemas recited against them during synagogue worship. Jerusalem, which had enjoyed a brief period of independence, had fallen and been destroyed. It is easy, in dark times, to give in to hopelessness and despair.

Although the words that begin the Gospel of John acknowledge the darkness, they are shot through with images of light. These ringing words have thrilled the hearts of Christians throughout the ages, as they have struggled with their own times of darkness. In the midst of darkness, God has been revealed. Again and again darkness and evil will try to take over but always the light of God has shone, piercing the darkness and bringing hope. God has shone a light that could never be overcome. In the life of Jesus of Nazareth, light was brought to all people, for he was no ordinary man. He was the Word of God.

Because of God's decisive act, the darkness could never again be complete. As difficult as that time in which the gospel was written might seem, something new had occurred, and the darkness had experienced its final defeat. In darkness, from now on, a light would shine, a light that could never be overcome, and that light would shine for all people. "The true light, which enlightens everyone" had come into the world (John 1:9). We don't have to fear the darkness anymore for in that darkness Christ has been revealed. We are no longer strangers lost in the darkness, but we are children of the light. "From his fullness we have all received, grace upon grace" (John 1:16).

Darkness and Light

The image of a light shining in the darkness is a powerful one. The other evening, my family and I lost our power for about an hour. When the lights went out it was very dark. Stumbling and tripping, I finally managed to find a flashlight. With it I had enough light to locate some candles and candlestick holders. The candles in the darkness provided a much-needed function. By candlelight, we could move safely about. By candlelight, we could read. By candlelight, we could see each other's faces. It is amazing what one candle or two can do to banish the darkness. And yet, without the darkness surrounding it, the light of a candle does not seem special. When the moon shines in the day, it is a faint echo of its nighttime self. A lamp on in the daytime can remain unnoticed: the far greater light of the sun makes its light unnecessary. I will sometimes forget that I have a candle lit during the day but in the darkness I clearly see the power of its light.

It doesn't take a very big light to push back the darkness. It takes only a small candle to make it possible to move safely through the darkness. Even a small flame provides heat and comfort along with the light. As powerful and strong as darkness is, light can vanquish it, perhaps not completely but at least in the surrounding area.

And in darkness, we look for those sources of light. We stumble around in dark rooms, groping for light switches to banish the darkness. We light candles during power outages to push back the darkness. Dark and dangerous shorelines have lighthouses to provide a safe passage for ships. In dark tunnels, we strive to make out the light that signals the end of the darkness. Camping in the wilderness, we light fires as much for the light as for the warmth. In the darkness, we are much more aware of the power of light.

And in our times of spiritual darkness, we look longingly and sometimes frantically for light. We hope to find at least a sliver of light, a glimpse that can relieve our inner darkness, for light in the darkness gives hope. Where there is light, there is life.

God as Light in the Darkness

The prophet Isaiah proclaimed "the people who have walked in darkness / have seen a great light; / those who lived in a land of deep darkness—/ on them light has shined" (Isaiah 9:2). But darkness was not confined to the time of Isaiah, and God's light has shone through many a time of darkness. It is perhaps no surprise that the followers of Jesus found this image a way of explaining what God was doing in Jesus. Into their darkness, God had sent a new light into the world, bringing light to everyone.

But was that light really powerful enough to overcome the darkness? The crucifixion of Jesus seemed to have extinguished any glimmer of hope, and it seemed as if darkness had overcome the light of God's self-revelation. For those who had followed Jesus, it would certainly have seemed that darkness and death were more powerful than the light brought by the one who was known as the Christ, God's anointed one. I doubt whether you could have found anyone after the crucifixion and death of Jesus who would have believed that this light could once again challenge the darkness.

On Wednesday of Holy Week, we do the service of Tenebrae. The word *tenebrae* means "shadows," and the service marks the gathering darkness of Holy Week. As the service progresses, more and more candles are put out, and the darkness grows. Near the end, the final candle is hidden, as Jesus is hidden in the tomb. But the candle doesn't stay hidden. Although it looks as if the darkness has won, it is a short-lived victory. Just before the service ends, the candle is brought out, to illuminate the darkness again. It is not a big light, but it does pierce the darkness and reminds us that no matter how dark things get, God sends light into our own darkness. God is present even in the darkest times.

Like the light that shows more brightly in the night, sometimes it is really easier to find God in the darkness. When all is going well, we may not notice the extra brightness of God's presence. We may not realize how dependent we are upon God's presence. But in the darkness we are reminded of our absolute dependence upon God's light, the source of our hope and our life.

Illuminating Our Darkness

Walking out onto the balcony of a friend's cottage overlooking the lake, I don't immediately see stars in the sky. My eyes have been blinded by the light. It takes some time outside to see in the darkness once again. But I have learned to wait; otherwise I can miss the stars in the sky. The light is there, but sometimes, in the darkness, it takes time to find it.

That is also what I have found with my times of darkness. When I first enter the darkness, I can see no light. The eyes of my heart have been blinded by the stronger light, and the fainter glimmers in the darkness do not register. In time, however, if I wait, if I keep looking, if I have faith, light begins to appear. Often the light is faint at the beginning. I may not be sure that it is present. Like a faint object in the night sky, the light may require me to avoid looking directly at it in order to see it. It may be visible only out of the corner of my eye.

But patience is rewarded. The darkness is not complete. Our eyes can learn to find the light in the darkness. As we are reminded in the first chapter of John's Gospel, the light is shining in the darkness, and the darkness has not and will not overcome it.

In our times of darkness, it can be difficult to remember that. In our times of darkness, it can be hard to continue to peer into the blackness, searching for any glimmer of light. In times of darkness, it can be very difficult to be patient, to wait for our eyes to adjust so that we can see the faint glimmers. John assures us, however, that the light cannot be swallowed by the darkness. In the darkness God's light shines, a light that is life for all.

And that light shining in the darkness has great power. It has the power to restore hope. It has the power to transform us into children of God. Most of all, it has the power to reveal the glory of God. "The true light, which enlightens everyone, was coming into the world" (John 1:9). It may not make our initial wait in the darkness any easier, but it means that our waiting is well worth it.

Questions for Discussion

1. When do you first remember hearing the prologue to the Gospel of John (John 1:1-18)? How did you understand its images of light and darkness at that time? Has there been a change in your understanding of those images of light and darkness?

2. When have you had to wait for the eyes of your heart to become accustomed to the darkness in order to see the faint glimmers of light? When in your life has waiting in the darkness been rewarded?

3. As you waited in the darkness, what gave you hope?

4. What does the image of light in the darkness reveal to you about Jesus Christ?

CHAPTER TWELVE

The Night Is as Bright as the Day: Embracing the Darkness

(Psalm 139:7-12)

Even the darkness is not dark to you;
the night is as bright as the day,
for darkness is as light to you. —Psalm 139:12

I have come a long way since seminary, when I wondered if the darkness that I experienced was due to a lack of faith. In fact, those times of darkness have brought me closer to God. They haven't been easy. Some have been incredibly painful, but in each case, I have been pushed into a new relationship with God, one based less on what I could actually see and more on what I could experience in other ways. Although I can't say that I enjoy times of darkness, I no longer fear them in the same way, for I have learned that in them and through them, God is present.

In this understanding I stand with a whole range of characters from the Bible who have also found God in the darkness. Included in this list are the psalmist, Abram, Saul, Jacob, Joseph, Nicodemus, and even Jesus. It is a distinguished company, and if I have something in common with these characters, perhaps I have discovered something important.

As I began to see that darkness as something not to be feared but to be accepted and even embraced, I found others who had shared in that experience. Few people talk about embracing the darkness. Far too often Christianity is seen as unending light; only those who have limited faith allow any darkness to creep in. But darkness is just as much a part of our lives as light. God made both the darkness and the light. By denying a place in our faith for darkness, we are limiting the ways in which we can encounter God. I know that my life and my faith have been richer because of the combination of light and darkness. Times of darkness contrast with times of joy, and it is that combination of light and dark that enriches our lives.

It is not hard to celebrate times of great light, and we naturally find others to share in our joy. We are eager to spread the news of what is happening. We can scarcely contain our delight. Filled with joy, we may not notice the empty place within us that can be filled only by God; and with others around us, we may have trouble hearing God. In the darkness of silence, on the other hand, other voices are quieted, and we are better able to hear God.

It was in one such time that I went on an individual silent retreat. In the lodge where I was staying, there was a small chapel. The stained glass windows were small with darker, more abstract shapes within them. When I first entered the chapel, it was evening, and the sun was setting. Some light was coming in through the windows but it was dim, and I found that I preferred to sit in that semi-darkness. I felt at home in the darkness.

As I sat there, it got darker and darker until the only light coming through the windows was from a security light outside. It didn't provide much illumination—yet somehow it seemed too much. I moved to sitting on the floor, where I could not see even that small amount of light. I was enveloped by the darkness.

I don't know that I had any great revelation in the darkness. I certainly didn't solve all of my problems but sitting on the floor of the chapel I felt wrapped in the darkness. The darkness wasn't a threat but somehow it had instead become like a warm and sheltering blanket. It felt womblike and comforting. I felt at home there in a way that I had not felt at home in the bright lights.

Most of all, I felt God's presence. It was nothing that I could see. I could not grab it and hold onto it. I couldn't manipulate it any way. The air of the place was filled with the sense of God's presence, and that presence surrounded and penetrated me.

George Fox, in his journal, says, "For I saw that there was an ocean of darkness and death, but an infinite ocean of light and love which flowed over the ocean of darkness."[1] In that darkness I was aware, in a way that I am often not aware, of the light and love that was flowing through that ocean of darkness. I need the darkness to become aware of the light and of the love flowing over it.

The psalmist says of God, "Darkness is not dark to you; / the night is as bright as the day; / darkness and light to you are both alike" (Psalm 139:12 BCP). This scripture reminds me that it is not for God's sake that I encounter the darkness. Darkness and light are irrelevant to God but not to me. I need the darkness in order to grow closer to God. Perhaps I am like a night-blooming flower that requires darkness to open my blossoms. In the darkness, I am more fully open to the One who has created me.

The darkness has many gifts to offer us if we are willing to enter it. There are painful and scary things in the darkness but there is also creation and rebirth. There is promise and enlightenment. There is transformation and revelation. Most of all, in the darkness we may encounter the God for whom darkness and light are both alike. T. S. Eliot, in his poem "The Four Quartets," counsels us to wait in stillness and without expectation for God to turn the darkness into light. "But the faith and love and hope are all in the waiting. . . . So the darkness shall be the light, and the stillness the dancing."[2]

It is hard to imagine that darkness could be light and stillness could turn to dancing but we have a God who delights in turning all upside down. Having experienced that reversal a few times in my life, I am willing to be still and wait in the darkness, knowing that in the darkness God is present.

In the end, it really doesn't matter whether I am in darkness or light, for God is everywhere. In the darkness, as the world around me dims, however, I can "see" God more clearly. In the darkness, God dazzles me, an experience shared by Henry Vaughan in his poem "The Night." "There is in God (some say) / A deep, but dazzling darkness."[3]

Pray that all of us experience that night, in that deep but dazzling darkness, where we might be in God and where we might live invisible and dim.

Questions for Discussion

1. The Bible describes many different experiences of darkness. Of the ones that we have explored, which one(s)
seems to most closely reflect your own experience?
2. What are some of the treasures that you have found in
your times of darkness?
3. What would it take for you to be able to embrace the
darkness?

Notes

1. George Fox quoted in Thomas R. Kelly, *A Testament of Devotion* (San Francisco: HarperSanFrancisco, 1992), 67.
2. T. S. Eliot, section I, stanza 3, lines 26, 28 of "The Four Quartets: 2. East Coker" in *T.S. Eliot: Collected Poems 1909–1962* (New York: Harcourt, Brace & World, 1970), 186.
3. Henry Vaughan, stanza 4, lines 1-7 of "The Night" in *The Oxford Book of English Verse 1250–1918* (New York: Oxford University Press, 1940), 411.

Receiving Treasures of Darkness

I will give you the treasures of darkness
and riches hidden in secret places,
so that you will know that it is I, the LORD,
the God of Israel, who call you by your name.
—Isaiah 45:3

The chapel is not particularly old but it is constructed to convey great age. The walls are very thick. The stained glass windows are small, admitting only a little light. It is very dim, even in the daytime. As I open the door I come face-to-face with rows of vigil candles. Several are lit, casting their red glow. In the darkness, they shine strongly, and their light is welcoming.

I often go there to sit and to pray. For in this semi-darkness, I feel at home. I find that I now feel more at home in such subdued lighting than I do in brightly lit spaces. The dimness nourishes my soul, and I find myself searching for such dark and inviting places, for they are full of treasures and riches hidden secretly.

If anyone had told me years ago that I would find my home in darkness, I would have thought that they were joking. I felt much more drawn to the brightness and beauty of full daylight. Sunny days lifted my heart and soul and made them sing. Why would anyone choose the darkness?

And I do still appreciate a bright and beautiful day. I love the brilliant blue of the skies. I glory in the way the sunlight flashes off water and lights leaves from behind. When I see any of these things, I stop and give thanks for the beauty with which God has graced this world. And yet I often feel more at home in the dimness that seems to me to speak powerfully of God's mystery and presence. That has been, and continues to be, one of the treasures of darkness that I have received. Perhaps that is why I feel at home in the darkness: for in the darkness I have found God.

Augustine says that our hearts are restless until they rest in God. Resting in God: there is perhaps no better definition of home. Although I cannot stay in the darkness forever, I find that I need those times in order to do the work that I am called to do. In the darkness, I rest in God more easily. As Isaiah points out, there are indeed treasures of darkness and riches hidden in secret places. My wish and my prayer for you is that you find your home, both in darkness and light, the place where you can rest in God.